Educational Wellness

A Sensory Approach to Teaching and Learning
2nd Edition

Student Responses to Classes Using *Educational Wellness*

As a student who has experienced the Hilliard Circle of Teaching and Learning I have truly been impacted and inspired. If more teachers implemented sensory teaching in the classroom, student involvement and learning would skyrocket. *Educational Wellness* should be every teacher's handbook.

Lauren Elrod
Graduate, O'More College of Design

I really didn't know what to expect when I signed up for college classes; I haven't been in school since Noah and I first drew out the plan for the Ark in woodshop! I was pleasantly surprised to see the speech and composition classes I took that used the principles of *Educational Wellness* were not only informative, but fun. I actually looked forward to these classes instead of dreading them.

The classes were interactive and interesting, not simply lectures and assignments. Each assignment was unique and easy to understand, and if someone didn't understand it, the teacher was always willing to answer any questions we had. Also, the teacher let us email our work during the process, giving us guidance right until we had to turn in our final project. We were always graded on the total experience of the class, not just the paperwork. I believe this speech course prepared us for the world of business meetings, presentations, and corporate America, and to me, that prepares you for real life, not just the graduation walk. Because a degree with no knowledge of how to interact with the real world, is just an expensive piece of paper.

DeWayne Pulliam
Director of Security, O'More College Of Design
Student

Taking a class that taught these principles of *Educational Wellness* opened my eyes to a variety of different learning styles, and through this learning, I was also introduced to different tools that work best for me.

I wasn't considered a great student in high school, and I think it was mostly because I simply wasn't learning because of the way the information was being presented. School was a constant struggle for me. I spent countless hours in high school reviewing flash cards and cramming for tests, only to do average at best, not because I wasn't smart, but because I didn't understand the information in the first place, and I am not good at conventional test taking.

After hearing there are different ways to learn, I was able to decide which worked best for me, such as sensory learning, connecting the lessons to daily activities, and evaluating using alternative methods (all presented in this book). Once I knew the Hilliard Circle of Teaching and Learning, I was able to ask my teachers questions differently and was able to comprehend their answers, bringing me to a higher level of education: not only by better learning the information presented to me by the teacher, but also by learning about myself.

Amber Elardi
Graduate, O'More College of Design

The Educational Wellness class is one of the most memorable courses I have taken. I loved learning about the various aspects of teaching, learning, and education. It hadn't occurred to me before to incorporate our physical senses to further engage learning. I have always known I'm a visual learner, but I learned from Dr. Hilliard that I can certainly benefit from utilizing my other senses in a learning environment. Not only was *Educational Wellness* helpful to me as a student, but it has been useful as a parent as well.

Emily Husbands
Former Student, O'More College of Design

Published by
Hilliard Press
a division of
The Hilliard Institute for Educational Wellness

Franklin, Tennessee
Oxford, England

www.hilliardinstitute.com

Educational Wellness:

A Sensory Approach to Teaching and Learning
2nd Edition

Dr. K. Mark Hilliard
Professor Jessa R. Sexton

Dedication

I dedicate my portion of research and writing to my grandparents:

Jack and Lola Hilliard, whose continual pride gave me great strength;

Ruzelle C. Jones, whose tattered copy of *Gone with the Wind* binds me forever to our shared love of literature; and

Charles L. Jones, whose addiction to education runs through my veins, who still inspires me towards constant personal study.

Jessa R. Sexton

I dedicate my portion of the book to my parents, Jack and Lola Hilliard, who did not listen to me when, as a teenager, I argued the value of them allowing me to skip college to use the money for what I considered a wiser investment—a sports car. Instead, I opted for a 1965 Plymouth Valiant and a college education. My parents were my inspiration for learning with passion. I still love you both dearly and cherish the gift of learning, well instilled.

K. Mark Hilliard

We both would like to dedicate this second edition to Deidra Hilliard Beene, sister and aunt to the authors, who loved education as we do and passed far too early from this earth.

Special Thanks

We must give our appreciation to our friends at Harris Manchester College, University of Oxford: Dr. Ralph Waller, Dr. David Wood-fine, Sue Killoran, and Helen Passey. Your assistance with research as we were blessed to study at Harris Manchester is woven into the fabric of this book.

Table of Contents

Abstract

No matter the preference in teaching style, educators must recognize that learning takes place in both the cognitive mind and the intuitive spirit. Unless we first accept the student as he is—an analytical, logical, scientific learner or a creative, intuitive, artistic learner—we will continue to fail in our attempts to make the educational process all-inclusive. We must no longer acknowledge one gift or intelligence while excluding the other. We must concede that the arts and the creative avenues for teaching and learning are as significant as the sciences and the logical educational processes connected with education. And we must recognize that a well-balanced teaching and learning philosophy and experience will reach most students today and tomorrow.

The *Educational Wellness* philosophy is designed to attain the post-didactic balance through a comprehensive, wholistic model for instruction and learning that integrates the sharing of individual experiences of both teacher and pupil; employs a multiplicity of teaching and learning styles based on sensory teaching and learning, sensory awareness, and channeled sensory perception; engages students in high-level, critical thinking; researches and applies alternative methodologies for teacher and student assessment within a specific populace or identified intelligence; constructs a unique physical and psychological campus and classroom environment; and analyzes and reconstructs the facets of the lecture to make it a viable teaching tool—all of which collectively creates an educational atmosphere conducive to highly individualized teaching and learning.

Purposes

Purposes of Learning

The initial purposes of learning are to gain the information and skills needed for basic goals:

- *surviving;*
- *surviving and caring for our family and friends;* and
- *becoming productive and marketable*—to be able to provide something of economic value.

On a higher level, the purposes of learning are to gain the information, skills, and desire to achieve more significant goals:

- *living a productive and socially meaningful life;*
- *excelling in productivity and meaning for our personal society and culture;* and
- *excelling in productivity and meaning* not only for our personal society and culture, but for the *society and world at large.*

The ultimate goal is that, in our excellence, we will find meaning and purpose for ourselves and others—to become the best we can be at whatever we do.

Purposes of Higher Education

The initial purposes of higher education are often goals connected to gaining a career:

- obtaining a *degree/diploma*;
- establishing *credibility* within an academic area;
- *increasing knowledge and skills*;
- assuring a specific level of *mastery of knowledge and skills*; and
- increasing our ability to *utilize the knowledge and skills in a meaningful and marketable fashion.*

More advanced purposes allow teachers and learners to see the ability of higher education to aid a student in attaining further-reaching goals:

- increasing our ability to *think critically and creatively*;
- increasing our ability to *think individually*;
- gaining opportunities that *expand personal experience*;
- *increasing world awareness* (local, national, and international);
- creating a desire and pattern for *lifelong learning*;
- gaining the desire and ability to *become responsible citizens*; and
- *increasing cultural, religious, and political awareness and sensitivity.*

The ultimate goal of higher education is to take the gifts and talents with which we have been blessed, to grow and expand these gifts and talents, and to increase our desire to seek or create opportunities to share our gifts and talents with others.

Preface

Jessa Sexton

I have felt honored to work on this project with my fellow teacher, my friend, my father, Dr. K. Mark Hilliard. His asking for my help with the book and our time together in research, observation, and conversation over the past eight years has been a time of great growth in my career and in our relationship.

Educational Wellness began as a presentation Mark gave for the Oxford Round Table in the summer of 2006. The sixteen-page paper developed and grew as he furthered his research on the elements of that presentation: the **Five Primary Pedagogical Elements of Educational Wellness** shared in this text. We later worked on and added to this edition a sixth element: the art of the lecture.

As a teacher, I have used the methods and ideas described throughout this book. The foundation of this text stems from Mark's time in what could be described as his *educational meditation* or *academic philosophizing*. (These moments occur during conversations with students or other educators, his personal readings of classic philosophers, and personal reflections over his morning hot tea.) Because we have often written of our experiences in first person, I have added my name to any subtitle before a section of my own creation. Any subsection without my name is Mark's. Hopefully this will keep you, the reader, clear on who has written what.

I come from a family of educators. My father, brother, and both grandfathers have all taught various subjects including wellness, religion, music, chess, law, and more. My mother was the quiet editor who guided me through corrections of countless papers during my time as an English major. My grandmothers led Bible studies and taught others through example. With pride and a great heritage of learning Mark and I also teach.

We hope this book will inspire you to create meaningful classroom experiences, making learning engaging for your students and for yourself.

Introduction

I feel my initial responsibility with a topic like this, especially in an academic setting, is to help the audience expel any fear or skepticism associated with the terms *wellness* and *wholistic*. I do, however, quickly agree that this skepticism is a just concern because of the host of charlatans currently practicing under the pretense of wholistic wellness.

True wellness is a medical education term associated with the well-being of the whole person. I define it as a degree of wholistic health only achieved when an interconnected harmony exists between the various components of our human existence. This human continuum involves the mind (our intellectual processes and our emotions); the body (our physical condition relating to nutrition, physical adjustments, and physical activities); social interaction (our relationships); and the spirit and soul (our intuitive nature, creative spirit, and metaphysical belief systems).

In education, wellness involves *whole* learning: right and left cerebral hemisphere learning, creative and analytical learning, experiential and tactical learning, and knowledge gained through both the sciences and the arts. The term *wholistic* simply implies the methodology through which wellness, or educational wellness, occurs—a training of the whole individual through the use of the creative strengths of the arts and the reasoning aspects of the sciences.

As caring teachers, we must realize that our students come into the classroom from diverse socioeconomic and otherwise broad-based environmental, empirical, and educational backgrounds. If we self-limit our teaching styles and our subject matter only to those we find comfortable, we also limit learning. Whole teaching and learning must encompass critical *and* creative thinking, requiring an acceptance of both logical reasoning *and* intuition. (For perhaps intuition is sometimes a product of previous conscious or unconscious reasoning or learning.)

Whole teaching and learning necessitates a degree of understanding in both the arts and the sciences and the processes presented by both in obtaining educational meaning and purpose. This style also provides opportunities for all of the senses to become engaged in the learning process by using a multiplicity of teaching styles. Whole teaching aids students in determining their prominent learning styles. It also expands individual alternative approaches toward learning, helping learners develop methods that make up for personal learning difficulties. Whole teaching and learning takes place at the point where self-expression and critical evaluation find mutual acceptance, where intuition and reason unite, where art and science collaborate, and where all the senses are brought to conscious awareness.

Our ambition as teachers should be fivefold:

- to engage our students in this whole teaching and learning process as early as possible;
- to build confidence in their unique abilities to learn;
- to provide direction, meaning, purpose, and focus for their lives;
- to enhance and increase their individual skills and knowledge; and

- to create a desire within them to identify and utilize their distinctive skills and knowledge to benefit not only themselves, but the community in which they live and society in general.

This is education at its pinnacle—education by design.

Educational Wellness

What, then, is the avenue through which we, as educators, can best achieve this ambitious endeavor? A methodology I have entitled *Educational Wellness* is a course of action that unifies the creative discipline of the arts and the formal structure of the sciences. *Educational Wellness* is a strategy that creates the concept of *design* or *design education*.

And what is design? Design is art with intent; the unity of art and science; art transferred from thought, to form, to function. A teacup that just sits unusable on a shelf for its beauty is art; if one can take that cup and drink from it, it has design. The process of moving from art to design requires the artist to delve deeply into formulas, textures, chemicals, history, culture, psychology, and other various fields of science that might assist with the aspect of meaningful function. The artist then applies the science to the art and, in so doing, creates design.

Educational Wellness embraces six primary pedagogical elements that collectively create an educational atmosphere conducive to highly individualized student learning. This method is a comprehensive and wholistic philosophy of teaching and learning which incorporates the use of all the senses in the classroom, including those seldom applied—touch, smell, taste, and the sense of the spiritual. The approaches of *Educational Wellness* encourage students to aspire to improve themselves, to expand their gifts and talents, and to share these talents as the ultimate goal of learning, rather than to simply memorize and repeat information—the unexceptional goal presented by common rote learning.

Six Primary Pedagogical Elements of Educational Wellness

This philosophy was created with five major objectives:

1. integrating the sharing of individual experiences of both teacher and pupil;
2. employing a multiplicity of teaching and learning styles based on sensory teaching and learning, sensory awareness, and channeled sensory perception;
3. engaging students in high-level critical thinking;
4. researching and applying alternative methodologies for teacher and student assessment within a specific populace or identified intelligence; and
5. constructing a unique physical and psychological campus and classroom environment.

As I continued my teaching and personal research, I found a sixth valuable objective:

6. analyzing and reconstructing the facets of the lecture to make it a viable teaching tool.

These elements collectively create an educational atmosphere conducive to highly individualized and creative teaching and learning—whole learning, or *Educational Wellness*.

Mark and Jessa with Ralph Waller, Principal of Harris Manchester College, University of Oxford, after a meal together

Chapter 1
Expressions of Self
the sharing of individual skills, knowledge, and experiences of both teacher and pupil

Practicing Professionals

While I recognize that book knowledge provides an educational foundation, only experiential learning on the part of the teacher provides the ability to share authentic understanding. Teachers must first experience their own learning before they can effectively share it, and students must explore their learning through exposure to real-life situations in which they use the skills they are developing. The teacher, therefore, brings the marketplace into the classroom through past and present experience, but also takes students into the marketplace for bona fide learning. Upon returning to the classroom, both students and teachers can share both knowledge and experience.

Educational Expansion

Jessa Sexton

For any educator, this task of remaining plugged into the real world can be a daunting challenge. Still, personal growth in our disciplines is not an impossible task and is a necessary duty not only to our students, but also to ourselves. As my grandfather, Jack Hilliard, wrote in his last book, "The most successful teachers realize they do not know it all and continue to learn by studying and increasing their own ability to teach" (223). Author and long-time educator Parker J. Palmer explains, "Academics often suffer the pain of dismemberment...deeper down, this pain is more spiritual than sociological: it comes from being disconnected...from the passions that took us into teaching" (21). These passions include the love of teaching, of learning, and of a particular subject. We cannot disconnect ourselves from any of these, or we will lose our academic zeal.

As an English teacher, subscribe to the *New Yorker* to keep up on current trends in creative and essay writing, attend poetry readings and writers' workshops, and, of course, read and write for yourself on a consistent basis. William Zinsser confesses in his book *On Writing Well*, which any English advocate should read, "A writer will do anything to avoid the act of writing" (19), yet, if you are a writing instructor, you will not remember the challenge of this act unless you do it right along with your students.

If you teach science or health, read scientific journals, watch documentaries about the latest findings in your field, become involved in the world of science by taking a walk or camping in nature, arrange to view a medical procedure first-hand, or volunteer at a research center at your local college or medical facility.

History, music, theatre, and art teachers should visit museums, peruse bookstores for new material pertaining to your field, and attend a variety of styles of musical performances and concerts. Challenge yourself further by placing your work in a gallery, giving or collaborating in a performance, or speaking publicly.

Sometimes we forget the importance of sharing our talents with more people than just our students and in more places than just our classrooms.

As a math teacher, walk around the supermarket and take note of how retailers price objects in ways that often trick consumers; also, create and maintain a personal budget: the sharing of these real-life math-moments are the answer to the age-old student query, "When am I going to need to know how to do this?" On an even deeper and more personally and professionally edifying level, consider seminars. Dr. Jeremy Brazas values personal research and traveling to, and even presenting at, math conferences. These experiences, he explains, "keep me up to date in the field, open me up to ideas other people are having which can often help me with my own work, introduce me to people with similar interests, and help me promote my own work."

Dr. Brazas shares other ways for any educator to continue cultivating his skills and knowledge:

- Actively seek out and confront advanced or challenging problems. This could be at the research level or just challenge problems for advanced students.
- Keep learning as much as you can. You never know when a certain concept or technique might be useful in your own work. There is so much interesting stuff out there and so little time.
- Talk to others about their interests.
- Talk about your own work, interests, and about problems that are currently stumping you. Expressing it helps you understand it better and promotes your personal "brand."
- Seek the advice and help of more experienced professors.

If you haven't already, you should write up your educational philosophy; at the end of each school year, I suggest you modify that philosophy as you ruminate on the experiences of those semesters, the new skills and knowledge acquired through professional development, and the counsel of other educators. Not only will this document be ready for any future professional need, it will also become an active summary of you, the teacher and ever-learner.

While I am polishing and refining this second edition, I stay home with my three children under the age of five; I generally have dinner on the table at least five nights a week; my house is rarely a complete disaster; I homeschool my pre-kindergartener; I am working with my father on projects through The Hilliard Institute; and I will be teaching (only) one adjunct learning support writing class this upcoming semester. Though I am not in the typical classroom full time at the moment, I still understand the strains of keeping all things together—and the added tension of adding personal professional development to that long list. However, as teachers, when we actively involve ourselves in our subject outside the classroom, we develop the passion needed to inspire students inside the classroom.

Getting to Know Each Other

Mark Hilliard and Jessa Sexton

The sharing of experience required for educational wellness involves the teacher getting to know each student individually—personal background, the way a student thinks and learns, the personal dreams and desires, the particular likes and dislikes. Teachers are able to become effective models for individual learning if they know the individuals they are teaching.

Likewise, students need to get to know each other and have access to information about their teachers—especially their qualifications and experiences in the discipline being taught. We have found that those teachers we learn from the most are those teachers we know the most about: those teachers we feel are knowledgeable, experienced, well-trained, and willing to share their talents and experiences.

This sharing may take place through the syllabus, a question and answer period between students and teachers, or an introductory e-mail or letter to students from the teacher. Students may complete a simple questionnaire about themselves: things they enjoy doing, academic interests, past experiences, and future goals.

Jessa spent some time asking present teachers, college graduates, present college students, and high school students ranging in age from teens to forties the following questions: what makes a teacher "bad," and what makes a teacher "good"? Their replies overwhelmingly related to the topics in this section: passion, profession, and connection. These answers prompted her to ask how teachers can go about making connections with their students. Most of the answers overlapped, but a few stood out as being cleverly worded or rather thoughtful; these statements we have credited to the speaker by placing his or her name in parentheses. We think you will find these responses helpful in your endeavors to become a better professional educator.

Bad Teachers

- are boring / lack passion
  - sound monotone
  - seem uninspired
  - appear unenthusiastic and unexcited
  - don't want to be at school
  - seem unmotivated
  - cannot keep students' attention
  - dislike their jobs
- appear unknowledgeable
- show no sense of humor / are always serious
  - stay set in their ways
  - remain strict about everything
- lack control of class
  - yell or lose their temper
  - become easily frustrated
- give poor presentation and/or assessment of the material
  - go too quickly
  - talk over our heads
  - frequently get off topic

- go strictly by the book
- don't give clear assessment expectations
- are unorganized
- have no imagination
- give too much busy work
- "do not create an environment of learning" (Clay Alumbaugh)
- are unhelpful
  - appear to say, "figure it out yourself" (Crystal Kaker)
  - are hard to communicate with
  - leave us confused
  - won't put forth an effort to help us understand
  - give late or no feedback
  - offer no one-on-one help
- sport a bad attitude
  - make us feel stupid
    - if we ask a question
    - if we get an answer wrong
    - "I'd rather get a lower grade than feel stupid" (Katie Swain).
  - have no patience
  - are rude
  - play favorites
  - create an obvious separation / disconnect from students
    - are unfriendly
    - act as though students are an inconvenience
    - remain distant

Summary: Students label teachers as "bad" who appear boring and without passion and lack knowledge of their subject, have poor classroom management skills, cannot present the material of the class in a usable or understandable manner, are unhelpful, lack humor, and present attitudes that make the students feel unimportant or stupid.

Good Teachers

- are passionate / have fun teaching
  - make learning fun (mentioned by many)
  - enjoy their job
  - are motivated for what they're teaching
  - alternate activities and teaching styles
  - exhibit creativity
  - relate learning to real life
- conduct practical teaching
  - give good notes
  - have a straight-forward approach
  - are able to answer questions and explain (in more than one way)
- connect with students
  - know what is happening in our lives
    - take this into consideration in how they present the material
  - talk to us about things other than school
  - have a caring nature
  - connect emotionally with students
  - tell personal stories
  - care not just about how we are doing in class, but how we are in general
  - connect activities to students' interests
  - have a personality that is "friendly with authority" (Becca Osborn)
- exhibit a flexible attitude
  - remain flexible when possible
  - "swing with their students" (Jennifer Shipley)
  - "And they do it with all the passion of an Artist, the dedication of a Firefighter, and the salary of a fast food worker!" (DeWayne Pulliam)

Summary: Students want passionate teachers who can be flexible, use humor, mix up their teaching styles, are helpful and able to explain things, connect with students on various levels, and relate what students are learning to their lives and the real world.

Suggestions on how teachers can connect with students

- Attitude
  - be "friendly, but not fake" (Michelle Khokhlov)
  - show kindness
  - use humor
  - be approachable
  - make us want to come to school, not just because we have to
- Communication
  - talk to us (mentioned many times)
    - on our level
    - early on in class
    - about educational problems
    - about what we like
  - listen to us
  - give us ways to contact you easily
  - ask questions
  - ask if we have questions
- Association
  - link what we are learning with
    - our lives
    - things we know about
    - your personal stories
    - something we like
  - find common interests that we share
- Connections
  - educationally—know our strengths and weaknesses.
  - personally—find out our likes, dislikes, goals, and dreams.
  - distinctly—understand your students are different: "Spend time with me. I am not like the student next to me" (Sarah Mullis).
  - separately—get to know the personality of each class and each section, and coordinate your teaching styles appropriately

Summary: Students suggest you connect with them through various means: have an attitude that shows you value them and your job; communicate with them about your life, your subject, and what is important to them; create connections between life (theirs and your own) and your subject; and take the time to learn who they truly are.

Expressions of Self:
The Oxford Experience

In my many visits to the University of Oxford, I clearly recognized the following three principles:

- the practice of hiring teachers who have experience as practicing professionals within their chosen fields;
- the importance in teachers continuing to expand their personal educational experience; and
- the benefit in teachers getting to know each of their students personally and students getting to know each other and their teacher.

Prior to my arrival for the Oxford Round Table in 2006, for which I was to present a paper on *The Art and Science of Wholistic Teaching and Learning* (a paper that developed into this book), and participating as a Visiting Scholar and Fellow in the Summer Research Institute, Harris Manchester College, University of Oxford, I received repeated e-mail and letter correspondence from program coordinators. These informal bits of communication began by introducing me to the people who would serve as my mentors, tutors, lecturers, and even support faculty and staff: information about who they were, their educational background, their professional background, and their relationship to the college.

The initial contact was followed by questions about me and the request for a photo. Then came questions about my studies: my needs, desires, and interests while in Oxford; my preference of access to multiple libraries and resources; and my wishes of whom I would like to meet while at the university.

Upon my arrival, I actually had a resource list of books and journals already pulled from the library computer data file, information about popular areas of interest at Oxford, brief information and a photo of each other member of the Round Table and Institute, and appointments for requested meetings. I felt great appreciation for those who had worked so hard to make me, a student and learner in this situation, welcome and ready to learn. Also, the personal engagement pre-established by their time and energy positively affected my learning.

This same process can be created, at least on some level, by each of us as teachers, either before we come to class to meet our students by simplistic methods such as e-mails or letters, or by questionnaires provided during the first week of classes and discussed in class as soon as possible thereafter.

Many times during each day while at Oxford, opportunities were provided for us to get to know the Oxford faculty as well as other Fellows of the Institute. Three daily meals together, the Seniors Common Room's availability for informal small group meetings, morning and afternoon teas, and planned group events were the norm. I found that these personal times allowed me to get to know people on an entirely different level from that provided while in the classroom together.

These planned and unplanned encounters reinforced my conviction that the individual sharing of experiences of both teacher and pupil is astronomically important in the process of whole teaching and learning. I came to any and all sessions already engaged to learn based on the fact that I knew and appreciated those who would lead the discussions, lectures, or tutorials.

The final note of worth for this section on the Oxford Experience and Expressions of Self relates to the timely responses always provided toward my inquiries and needs. Questions were answered either immediately or agreements were made to assist me in finding answers. Materials were provided within the day or the following day. And everything needed was at my ready disposal.

Once when Jessa asked about the train to Stratford-upon-Avon to see Shakespeare's birthplace, the Principal of Harris Manchester himself immediately left the room to call for a train schedule. Jessa kept the piece of paper with his scrawling of times and prices as a memory of how a person of great importance found great importance in her academic and personal needs.

The educational emotions experienced? I felt those responsible for my academic guidance saw me as an individual with individual needs and desires. I felt respected and valued. If our students feel that we value them, if we show interest and an ability to meet their needs or guide them in meeting their own needs, they will feel respected and important—they will feel ready to learn.

Final Thoughts—Expressions of Self

Jessa Sexton

Dr. Ruth Beechick writes, "A teacher who loves learning earns the right and the ability to help others learn." Author and educator William Arthur Ward writes, "The mediocre teacher tells. The good teacher explains. The superior teacher demonstrates. The great teacher inspires." Both quotes remind us: our passion for the craft of teaching and for our subjects cannot wane, or we will cease inspiring our students. In order to keep that passion alive, we must continue our own learning and personal and professional growth.

"The ability of an educator depends on two qualities: knowledge and attitude" (Hilliard 223). "Bad teachers distance themselves from the subject they are teaching—and in the process, from their students. Good teachers join self and subject and students in the fabric of life" (Palmer 11). We will not be able to teach effectively—to make profound connections between our students and our knowledge—if we do not first present an attitude that communicates we believe this connection is necessary and become excited to make the necessary efforts to ensure it happens.

Mark and Jessa outline the final elements needed for this book in the Tate Library at Harris Manchester College.

Chapter 2
Learning by Design

the employment of a multiplicity of teaching and learning styles directed by sensory teaching and learning, sensory awareness, and channeled sensory perception

Engaged Learning

The whole person approach to teaching and learning draws on a vast array of teaching and learning styles, but the sheer number of these approaches can seem overwhelming to a teacher wishing to expand his or her techniques. I believe, however, this seemingly immeasurable assortment of styles can be simplified in understanding by sensory connections:

- an association with our physical senses (seeing, hearing, tasting, smelling, touching and moving, and many cultures and individuals include the metaphysical or spiritual sensation);
- the sensitivity of our sensory awareness systems (our ability to acknowledge varied and specific sensory stimulants); and

- our degree of channeled sensory perception (how well we understand and make use of sensory information for meaningful learning).

Our first introduction to any learning experience begins with a sensory stimulus. At times there is a cognitive awareness of this stimulation. However, quite often it goes unnoticed, and, when unnoticed, it likewise goes unrequited. How then can we transfer sensory impression into mental cognition and, even further, transfer this cognition into physical form with function—channeled sensory perception?

Part of the answer lies in determining whether or not sensory learning is an automatic, voluntary response or an activated process of will and thought, a developed response. The senses appear to react in both of these ways, for why else would we taste something for the first time and dislike it? Without recognition of the flavor, how can we recognize a dislike?

At some level our sensory impressions are hardwired: a sensory pre-coding for certain things, a precognition. Yet, I would challenge that without will and thought, without structured (channeled) learning, our minds have a hard time discerning and even noticing sensory impressions. Without guidance these impressions provide little in the way of meaningful, usable cognition.

Our responsibility as teachers, in employing a multiplicity of teaching styles, can be demystified by simply introducing a variety of sensory stimulations for any topic and following a format entitled *The Hilliard Circle of Teaching and Learning* (explained in the next chapter). We learn not only to *present*, but to *represent* a sensory experience through our words, gestures, enthusiasm, activities, expressions, openness, laughter, and genuineness. In so doing, *we actually become* the sensory stimulus through our stories, analogies, hands-on projects, and other visual and auditory expressiveness.

During the course of this practice, the student begins to learn in a way that can never be accomplished by rote learning. In essence, the student becomes engaged in the learning experience through the teacher's use of sensory words, concepts, or illustrations created by these words, and the use of sensory activities that engage the student physically, mentally, and emotionally through practical application. In so doing, the student not only sees and hears the information, but he touches it, tastes it, smells it, or is otherwise, through sensory responsiveness, drawn into the process of teaching and learning. He is then guided through each additional stage in the Circle of Teaching and Learning process, moving from lower to higher levels of learning.

Identifying Sensory Exposure

Each sense has its own unique way of inspiring and teaching. By experiencing a multiplicity of smells, tastes, sounds, textures, images, and emotions, we learn more about ourselves and about the essence of our environment. We move beyond audio/visual representation into the inward reality: beyond the surface into the inner core. We learn how to *create,* not simply *reproduce or copy.*

As both teachers and students, the more we study, engage, and use our senses, the more we learn to emulate these senses through our presence, our creations, and our productivity. A great teacher has enough knowledge and excitement for his subject that his passion and delivery alone can touch all the senses of his students as he teaches—illustrious teachers become the multi-sensory stimulants that engage students into the teaching and learning circle.

A great teacher does not stop at this point, though. Rather, he finds ways to physically stimulate his students, letting them smell, taste, hear, touch, and see items connected to the lesson and engaging them immediately in their learning.

Another reason for applying sensory teaching and learning is that there are parts of the brain that act as gatekeepers and do not allow familiar information and familiar methods of teaching and learning to pass on to higher levels of the brain for processing. If we do not engage our students in the teaching and learning process, the information we share may never make it to the level of the brain where they can actively use the information or, in many cases, even recall what has been taught.

Sound

The sense of sound is one of the most complicated to explain because of the delicate auditory system involved. In simplistic form, think of what we hear as an auditory expression of movement and thought created by vibrations or sound waves. Vibrations created by words (formed by thoughts), various natural and man-made sounds (which include a range of tones and pitches), and movement.

Fundamentally, the ear interprets sounds as these vibrations pass through the outer ear canal, into the middle ear, and against the eardrum. Here, the eardrum vibrates three tiny bones in the ear that carry the vibrations to a part of the ear called the cochlea. Hair-like nerve endings then convert the vibrations into messages to send to the brain. Finally, the brain makes meaning of the messages and provides cognition of what is being heard ("Come to Your Senses").

Music is one of the most-used methods of applying structured sound to create a sensory response. Why is music such a powerful stimulus? It activates multi-sensory responses: it sensuously strokes a variety of our senses. Stories and literature are also strong sensory activators, in that expressive words can stimulate the sense of taste, touch, smell, sight, sound, and even the metaphysical and spiritual sense as the writer's imagery creates a clear moment the reader experiences through words and imagination.

Each of these prominent auditory stimulators is strongest if the *listener* has experienced the things being described, or expressed, and can re-experience them in his mind. But there is also a passion that can be added in vocal or musical delivery if the *presenter* has experienced the feelings, emotions, or activities expressed in the song, the story, or literary reading.

Sounds can often become *too familiar*—the way the teacher speaks, lecture style teaching, expression of common knowledge, rote teaching—to the point that the student tunes out the teacher, and the information is never processed by the higher levels of the brain. Students can even get into the habit of immediately tuning out specific teachers based on the teaching styles used or the quality of the voice. Also dialects, accents, speed of talking, and choice of words can cause a misunderstanding or lack of understanding. Students need time to process and ponder the words being spoken.

Words Associated with the Sense of Sound

music		
instrumental	*a capella*	
speech—language		
various languages	*accents*	*dialects*
cultural uses of words		
speech—emotional use of words (expressions of...)		
kindness	*praise*	*appreciation*
challenge	*fear*	
nature sounds		
wind	*rain*	*thunder*
water	*fire*	
animal and insect noises		
bark	*meow*	*caw*
moo	*the flap of bird wings*	
man-made or industrial noises		
machinery	*equipment*	*traffic*

Expressions of the Sense of Sound

loud	soft	quiet
sensuous	forceful	resonating
rhythmic	expressive	passionate
detectable	undetectable	grating
pleasing	in or out of tune	harmonious
monotonous	emotional (happy, sad, angry, fearful)	

Effective Teaching and Learning Methods for the Sense of Sound

- Use animation and self-expression in lectures.
- Read out loud, with passion, and use appropriate gestures to support your words.
- Have students read out loud or repeat information in their own words.
- Use a variety of words, expressions, analogies, examples, formulas, and stories—these reduce misunderstanding.
- Re-cap the lesson at the end of each session and at the beginning of the next session.
- Provide definitions; then have students create their own and share with the class.
- Use practicing professionals as guest speakers.
- Offer oral examinations or reviews.
- Require student presentations and oral reports.
- Use mock trials and debates.
- Provide panels of experts on various aspects of a topic.
- Create discussion groups of students with common interests.
- Provide individual or small group tutorials.
- Use modern audiovisuals or purposeful vintage audiovisuals.
- Create musical, rhythmic, and verbal games and activities.

- Provide question and answer sessions—ask questions, allow students to ask questions, have groups create questions, teach how to find answers, have students create and e-mail questions before each class.
- Have students follow the lesson with a study guide, or follow an oral reading in the book.
- Remove excess background noises.
- Apply appropriate acoustical classroom technology.
- Use play acting and role play.

When teachers read with passion, offer intense verbal expression, and use appropriate auditory activities, students become more involved in the lesson. In essence, the teacher becomes the sensory stimulation that opens the door for learning. Likewise, when students are required to verbally clarify or participate in group discussions, this added sensory sound element assists student engagement in the learning process. The use of multiple teaching styles, or multi-sensory stimulation, during any lesson of more than thirty minutes significantly prolongs the ability to maintain student connectivity.

An Experience in Sound

Jessa Sexton

- Students who have a hard time understanding poetry or Shakespeare often are clear on the reading's meaning once they hear an appropriate verbal delivery. The vocal inflection, proper pauses, and use of facial expressions and gestures combine to turn what first seems to be fancy words in short lines into a story.
- One of the best methods I have used in helping students edit their own work is to read, or have the students read, their papers out loud as they follow along. Many times a student will stop me because he hears the grammatical mistake. If a line "doesn't sound right," there is probably something wrong with grammar, punctuation, or something else that is inhibiting clarity.

In both of these instances, I have paired the sense of sound with the commonly-used sense of sight to guide my students towards understanding subjects they often find daunting.

Sight

Sight is another complicated sense to describe, but it can be condensed into this basic process:

- Vibrations of light (light waves/rays) enter through the pupil to the lens.
- The lens focuses the image (upside down) onto the retina.
- Nerve cells (called rods and cones) on the retina detect the image and send that image via the optic nerve to the brain.
- The brain flips the image right-side up and translates what is being visualized. ("Come to Your Senses")

What we see provides a visual representation, or orientation, within the brain of outward symbols, signs, forms, sizes, shapes, colors, textures, movements, wholes, parts, emotions, natural products, man-made creations, people, animals, or nature. These visuals may be recognized as pleasing or displeasing.

Along with sound, sight is one of the strongest senses involved in the learning process, but we must touch, taste, smell, or otherwise be drawn into and experience what we see in order to make that image real; without practical experience, what we see only remains a visual image.

True seeing, the art of seeing, involves a connection between the inward person (knowledge, past experience, beliefs, and cognitive and spiritual insight), the physical eye (the optic system), and the object being viewed. Far too often there is a disconnect, or blinded interpretation, caused by inappropriate insight, inept thinking or knowledge, beliefs without foundation, and either a lack of, or badly chosen, experiences. This type of *vision* can actually blind us from seeing something, or even someone, in the true form. Also, we can be either attracted to (or not attracted to) what we see, we can respond neutrally, or we can fail (deliberately or inadvertently) to acknowledge what is seen.

Light, one of the major visual activators, can be expressed as radiant light (created by the release of energy); reflective light (created when energy bounces off or is reflected by an object, creating white); or absorbed light (created when energy is absorbed by an object, creating black). When some light is absorbed and some is reflected, we see color. The field of color psychology provides multiple uses of various colors to affect mood, sensitivity, power, weakness, motivation, and general well-being. The color green and natural warm colors are consistently viewed as colors of balance and harmony, neither over- nor under-stimulating. And a warm red is perceived by many cultures (especially Native American) as a color that stimulates thought, energy, action, and creativity.

Words Associated with the Sense of Sight

perspective	glance	eyes
viewpoint	peek	gaze
positions	view	color
vision	forms	see
shapes	natural light	vision
distance		

Metaphorically we see

skill	talent	lack of talent
clearly	truth	error
a grey area	the seen	the unseen
something as black and white		

Expressions of the Sense of Sight

far	near	up
down	next to	in front of/behind
light	dark	bright
dim	vivid	clear
vibrant	unclear	hazy

blurry	shadowy	colorful
panoramic	beautiful	ugly
whole	sectioned	full-spectrum
black and white	radiant	still
movements		

Effective Teaching and Learning Methods for the Sense of Sight

- Provide meaningful, good quality handouts.
- Place important information on a white or chalk board.
- Use computers in the classroom.
- Use a variety of visually-stimulating reading materials.
- Give written exams and quizzes.
- Use object lessons.
- Require visual research projects.
- Employ visual games.
- Establish creative group projects—building, drawing, painting.
- Have students take photos or make photo journals.
- Solve puzzles.
- Show students how to map or circle to create definitions.
- Require students to journal.
- Require note taking.
- Use the educational modeling formula to introduce new skills.
- Share field trip experiences—create out-of-classroom activities.
- Offer a variety of colors, shapes, forms, and symbols.
- Provide natural or full-spectrum lighting.
- Offer visuals from various angles, perspectives, heights, and positions.
- Use show and tell.
- Provide multiple types of visuals and audiovisuals—illustrations, charts, art, and diagrams.

By actually seeing something they have heard about, students can confirm and validate their learning experience: seeing also helps validate personal insights. But there is also a benefit to having students determine whether or not there is a visual disconnect with other senses by having them see something, then touch, taste, smell, or otherwise become engaged with the visual elements to determine if each of the senses agrees with the others. For many students, touching visuals is imperative. By touching what we see, the items become real, and in the process of touching, we are able to insure the accuracy of what we think we see.

An element seldom used with visuals is to present them from various angles, perspectives, heights, and positions. In so doing, we offer a greater understanding of the complexity, or simplicity, of the elements.

Ultimately, our goal with visual stimulation is to help our students appreciate the beauty in the visuals all around them, for we tend to spend more time with that in which we see beauty. By looking for beauty, we examine and experience visuals on an entirely different level.

An Experience in Sight

Jessa Sexton

- PowerPoint presentations are a visual way to make note-taking easier. I have found that teaching grammar rules is easier if my PowerPoint slides have art that reflects what is being taught. For example, when I teach about grammar mistakes, I create images that show what the incorrect sentence is actually communicating; these often humorous pictures clarify and help with memory.
- To help students view grammar rules in their everyday lives, I bring in common household products with mistakes as well as products that apply rules appropriately. The goal of writing classes is not to quote rules but to identify and fix mistakes in the real world. Seeing what we learn in the text in a relatable manner helps students meet this goal.

Touch

You may remember from your high school science classes that the skin is the body's largest organ; thus, skin is also the largest sensory organ. The skin is made up of receptors that receive vibrations and send related information to the brain in response to touch, pressure, pain, pleasure, and temperature. These feelings are experienced once the brain makes meaning of the information (Davis and Palladino 111-113). Since the skin covers the body, the sense of touch is constantly being stimulated. Still, certain areas of skin are more receptive, or sensitive, than others because of a higher number of nerve endings ("Come to Your Senses").

Touch provides physical, external assurance of what we think we see, through bodily contact and personal involvement. This sense offers kinesthetic appreciation for, and proof of, shapes, forms, figures, textures, movements, and emotions. Touch requires someone or something to move and involves nerve-ending sensations through contact. The items we touch, or those that touch us, can be of regular shapes and forms or irregular shapes or forms. We may or may not recognize them and may or may not find pleasure in them. By touching and moving, we come into contact with the real world. Without touch and movement, we significantly limit our ability to learn.

Words and Expressions Associated with the Sense of Movement

vestibular (deals with the inner-ear, bodily orientation, and movement)		
up	down	around
forward	backward	sideways
oriented	disoriented	balanced
spatial	order	disorder
left	right	east
west	north	south
fast	slow	physical activity
dance	walk	jump

run	play	roll
push	pull	drive
kinesthetic (movement of joints, muscles, arms, legs, and the position of the body in space)		

Words and Expressions Associated with the Sense of Touch

soft	hard	cold
hot	wet	dry
smooth	rough	silky
coarse	hands	feet
shoulders	body	guide
direct	shape	texture
irregular	symmetrical	crooked
straight	square	round
sensuous	callous	hit
shake hands	pat	high five

Effective Teaching and Learning Methods for the Sense of Touch and Movement

- Offer dancing, hiking, jumping, walking, or running activities.
- Exercise and participate in gymnastics or sports.
- Play games and use physical education activities.
- Create scavenger hunts.
- Provide travel and field trip experiences.
- Encourage free and structured exploration.
- Construct competitive or non-competitive activities.
- Develop physical tasks and challenge activities.
- Role-play and develop theatrical plays.
- Build or create something.
- Offer art, drawing, or illustration activities.
- Provide educational modeling of activities.
- Require students to take notes or follow a study guide.
- Have students write, type, or journal.

- Have students collect and/or touch specific materials, objects, textures.
- Experience the human form through touch, movement, and personal expression.
- Use hands-on individual and group activities.
- Provide physical work opportunities such as internships, shadowing, on-the-job training, field trips, and apprenticeships.

Touch is one of the earliest ways children relate to and learn about their environment—they touch everything. In fact, students need to touch items to insure their reality. By touching things, they create a greater appreciation for the item involved.

The process of touching involves some of the most sensitive parts of the body and engages the largest sensory organism, the skin. This experience is a way to connect with someone or something in an especially personal and sometimes spiritual way.

Metaphorically, we want to "touch" all our students. By better understanding physical touch, we better know how to "touch," or engage, our students' sense of taste, smell, sound, sight, spirituality, and physical touch.

Likewise, any appropriate movement related to the subject matter can help strengthen the learner's experience. Movement exercises the body and the mind—it provides opportunities for wholistic teaching and learning to take place. Exploration activities and research projects automatically require touch and movement.

An Experience in Touch and Movement

Jessa Sexton

- I have students act out the uses of punctuation marks. This activity helps students physically experience their learning.
- Sheets from a giant Post-It pad are a good way to get students moving around. I have placed these pads around the room, posted questions about the text we are reading, and let groups walk around filling in answers. The movement of this

activity gets students out of the worksheet rut and gets them moving. Also, by creating a competition out of it, offering a prize to the group who answers all the questions first, students are encouraged to stay on task.

Smell

Davis and Palladino simplify the process through which we distinguish various smells, or odors, into the following three major steps involving the olfactory system, the system that makes *sense* of odors:

- First, air enters the nostrils where tiny hairs filter the air we breathe (no smells detected at this point).
- Next, the air travels deep into the nasal cavity where millions of receptors accept and transfer the messages carried in the air, through vibratory impulses, to the olfactory bulb.
- From here impulses are passed to the brain for interpretation. An important note is that this excursion into the brain involves traversing the limbic system—a part of the brain involved in emotional and memory storage and processing as well as motivated behavior such as aggression, hunger, thirst, and sexual activity. (109)

Remember, these interpretations are important in helping us distinguish what we are smelling. And because of the strong connection between smell, flavor, thirst, and hunger, these interpretations also aid in our enjoyment of, or aversion to, various tastes. In fact, the sense of smell appears to be stronger than taste and thereby strongly influences our ability to enjoy food. (Think of the effects of smoke in a restaurant on how the food tastes, the intensified flavor of food as smell is increased when we chew the food, or the effect of holding the nose while eating.)

Whereas taste requires the mixture of chemical molecules with liquid (often saliva in the mouth), smell requires the mixture of chemical molecules with air. So the air that first enters the nose is composed of a mixture of air and chemical molecules from the environment that, through the process of olfaction, will be detected as unique odors, smells, or scents. As humans, we can detect about ten thousand scents. The easier the molecules mix in the air, the easier they are to smell (such as gasoline and other liquid chemicals) (Davis and Palladino 109).

Throughout history, smell has been used (incense, fire, candles, sacrifices, smoking, etc.) as a ritualistic way of becoming spiritually involved in an activity. These smells are perceived as a representation of the inner quality, or essence—often as a representation of the spirit or soul of the item or animal from which they were created. What is the meta-physical process involved? Through intake of the scent, those involved in the ritual sense the inner quality (the spiritual quality) of something, and this perception has an effect on the one(s) doing the smelling. (This effect can be relaxation, excitement, motivation, irritation, or initiate recall. An intimate smell can create pain, pleasure, or fear.) This practice suggests that we can learn much about something by smelling it, if we have the ability to decode the message—which may occur consciously, subconsciously, unconsciously, or spiritually.

The sense of smell is most closely linked to memory and recall, not only of facts but also of experiences and emotions. Dr. Rachel Herz has found through her research that "memories evoked by our sense of smell are more emotional than memories evoked by our other senses, including sight, sound and touch" (qtd. in *Living Well with Your Sense of Smell*). Another unique aspect of olfaction is that the brain can be tricked into detecting a smell which is not present—except in the memory (recall). Through internal visualization (imaging) or auditory stimulation, a smell can be retracted and re-experienced. The more scents we have experienced in real life, the more scents we can re-experience through literature, art, and a variety of teaching and learning activities.

To use the sense of smell in the teaching and learning process, the teacher can incorporate actual smells that relate to specific learning, integrate odors which alter mood and emotion, or use words or visuals which activate the olfactory system through recall. A practical approach to this process is to have students study words associated with smell, then find meaning that relates a specific topic to a specific smell, and locate actual smells or olfactory representations, such as visuals to present to, and discuss with, the class.

Words Associated with the Sense of Smell

industrial odors	sewage	toilet
waste	skunk	body odor
animal odor	fire	smoke
candles	perfume	fragrance
soap	cleansers	herbs
liquor	food	cooking
baking	frying	death
decay	garbage	trash
tobacco	candy	aromatherapy
incense	essential oils	leather
paint	scent	sniff
whiff		
fabrics and material		
silk	cotton	polyester
chemicals		
ammonia	sulfur	gasoline
nature		
flowers	plants	trees
hay	coffee	tea
fruit		

Expressions of the Sense of Smell

pleasant	unpleasant	soothing
relaxing	aromatic	fresh
pungent	flowery	rotten
nauseating	rancid	intense

sensual	moldy	dirty
clean	damp	old
natural	new	mouth-watering
enticing	alluring	odorous
revolting	emotional	memorable
reflective	subtle	flavorful
weak	strong	

Effective Teaching and Learning Methods for the Sense of Smell

- Make sure the classroom has a pleasant smell.
- Incorporate the smells of the discipline (art: paint and supplies; math: calculators, money, erasers; English: books, paper, writing materials; science: formaldehyde, nature).
- Incorporate actual smells relating to the topic (war: gunpowder, smoke, mud) into the lesson.
- Identify the smells noted in a reading to connect students to the topic—have the students bring representatives of the smells to class.
- Create metaphorical representations using words associated with smell as applied to various situations—"that stinks," etc.
- Experience smells in the environment; then explore, locate, and identify each smell.
- List smells that relate to any chosen topic—do this as a game.
- Explore the positive effects of various smells on teaching, learning, memorization, creativity, etc.
- Examine negative smells in the environment, and determine how to address each smell.

The relationship of brain processing and the association to various smells and tastes can be used to activate memory, emotions, and behavior modification. Smells can trigger emotions either consciously, subconsciously, or unconsciously, making it a useful tool in the teaching and learning process—smells that relate to the lesson; smells that excite, motivate, or relax; or smells that activate memory.

Davis and Palladino write that the same part of the brain, "the *limbic system*, the emotional part of the brain," processes both odors and memories (110). This explains why the practice of detecting and remembering smells has been proven to assist with the ability to recall other data. There is an increase in activated memory when a specific smell is used during study and reapplied during assessment or testing (memory association). According to *Living Well with Your Sense of Smell*, "Researchers have even found that our ability to recall a specific scent surpasses even our ability to recall what we've seen. Dr. Trygg Engen found that people recall smells with a 65% accuracy after a year; by contrast, it is estimated that visual recall of photos sinks to about 50% after only four months!"

An understanding of smells and their effect is very important in setting up a teaching, learning, living, or working environment: how to avoid certain smells, secure them, enjoy them, and share them. Every subject, topic, job, and discipline has its own unique smells, and learning about these specific smells helps us better understand that with which we are involved. (See *Chapter 7* for examples.)

The spiritual implications associated with smell can help us in using ritualistic activity more effectively in both teaching and learning. In art, literature, food preparation, and a variety of other subjects, we are better prepared to be passionate in using the sense of smell if we have experienced this sense in a multiplicity of ways. And by understanding smells and odors, we better understand the metaphorical usages of words and phrases relating to smell (that stinks, the smell of money, the deal went sour).

An Experience in Smell

Jessa Sexton

- While going through a study guide with students, provide a particular (pleasant) scent in the room. Encourage them to study with that same scent, and then provide the smell again during the test.

- Smells are often incredibly symbolic in my field of study: literature. In "A Rose for Emily" by William Faulkner, decay (of the Old South, of the title character, of love) is portrayed through dust; this same smell reveals a similar symbol in James Joyce's "Eveline." Honing in on this sensory element while reading can disclose layers we might not notice otherwise.

Taste

As previously noted, the full sense of taste actually encompasses both the mouth (gustation) and nose (olfaction). Whereas the nose begins the process of deciphering the molecular message of molecules coming into contact with air, the mouth and taste involve the mixing of molecules and liquid. The mouth contains 10,000 taste buds, each having approximately twenty sensory receptors. While most of these taste buds are located on the tongue, some are also located on the throat and roof of the mouth. Individually, these sensory receptors are believed to distinguish between only simple classes of taste such as salty, sweet, bitter, and sour, but because more than one receptor cell can be activated at the same time, we can distinguish a multiplicity of flavors (Davis and Palladino 107-108).

As things come in contact with these sensory cell receptors, messages are sent to the medulla (a part of the brain which controls swallowing, throwing up, and breathing), then the thalamus (a vibratory message relay station), then on to the somatosensory cortex in the forebrain which identifies the flavor. Interestingly enough, this somatosensory area of the brain processes every sensation other than smell, which is processed by the limbic system ("Come to Your Senses").

The amount of taste bud receptor cells and their level of sensitivity diminish with age, which can help explain why we may end up enjoying tastes we did not like as a child. Another age-related factor is that these taste receptor cells are continually replacing themselves every few weeks throughout our life (Davis and Palladino 108).

The process of gustation begins when we first take something into our mouth:

- What goes into our mouth is either previously mixed with liquid, or the mouth provides the liquid via saliva.
- Once the mixture is in the mouth, we can begin to examine texture, form, shape, and size.
- We may then swallow the mixture, spit it out, move the mixture around in the mouth some more, or vomit it up as we attempt to swallow; our gustatory system may reject the objects.
- Just as with smell, any particular molecular mix may be liked or disliked, and the sense of taste is also believed to express the inner-essence of its provider (a plant, animal, liquid, solid, poison, etc.).

As teachers, we can use actual flavors and tastes in the teaching and learning process, or we can use words, visuals, and activities to express the sense of taste. Sharing a meal is a wonderful way to experience taste with our fellow learners—our students. These shared meals are a communion, a very personal sharing of ourselves with others, a sharing in a life-sustaining ceremony. This intimate level of communion may be realized consciously, or may remain subconscious or unconscious, but, either way, the sharing of food and tastes has a lasting relational effect on the participants (a meal with a date, eating with the family, eating with an employee or employer, eating with students or colleagues, eating with a group, eating with only one other person, etc.).

As a teacher, develop a list of tastes that relate to a discipline, or have students develop a list of tastes that relate to a topic or discipline. Use words that represent tastes and develop a line of clothing, book titles, paint colors, or rename laws or cities based on taste association.

Words Associated with the Sense of Taste

meat	vegetable	bread
pasta	oils	dessert
drink	alcohol	carbohydrates
fat	protein	liquid
charcoal	propane	toothpaste
mouthwash	many of the items also noted under smell	

Expressions of the Sense of Taste

sweet	sour	bitter
salty	hot	cold
spicy	sickening	pleasing
unpleasing	intense	subtle
mild	medium	sharp
succulent	good	bad
flavorful	bland	tangy
tasty	fiery	refreshing
dry	lukewarm	fishy
carbonated	fresh	canned
frozen	moist	fried
baked	raw	rare
well-done	grilled	

Effective Teaching and Learning Methods for the Sense of Taste

- Health and science: bring in examples of healthy and un-healthy foods.
- History and literature: have students eat the foods that would have been popular in the setting of your study.
- Art: let students eat different kinds of fruit before they draw them, or have students create color palettes based on their sensations as they eat various foods.

- Math: teach students the importance of fractions by making them use half or double (or use even more complicated fractions) recipes and letting them eat their product.
- History, foreign language, and literature: select, cook, and eat foods that relate to any topic or period of time.
- History and health: study, explore, and taste wild edible foods from your local area.
- Health and family and consumer science: invite a chef to the class to discuss food, flavors, and taste.
- Art and design: invite an artist or designer to the class to discuss metaphorical good taste.
- Any course: examine metaphorical uses of terms relating to taste and their origin.
- Health: have students explore the healthiest fast food, and then discuss the ramifications of fast food on humanity.
- Any course: consider the symbolic nature of any elements in the topic on hand; think outside the box to see if any of these relate to the sense of taste. Can you create a memorable classroom moment by incorporating that taste?

As in the case for smell, the relationship of brain processing and association to various tastes can be used to activate memory, emotions, and behavior modification. Various tastes (especially foods and food preparation) have important cultural and historic significance as well—by understanding the foods people eat, we better understand the people.

In the educational process, experiencing flavors increases our use of, and understanding of, descriptive language. In art and language, for example, we must experience a taste or flavor in order to best represent it with words or visuals, or to understand it as presented to us in visual form or as expressed by words. And as you might imagine, the relationship of taste and nutrition has significant educational implications. As we experience a variety of tastes, we simply better understand the things that provide the tastes.

Likewise, by understanding tastes and flavors, we better understand the metaphorical usages of words or phrases relating to taste (good taste, bad taste, a sweet kiss, the taste of death or life, to get a taste of something).

An Experience in Taste

Jessa Sexton

- Communication is key in education and in any career. The ability to describe and clarify is a useful skill for any learner. Giving a student a food, having that student fully experience the smells, tastes, and textures in his mouth, and then asking that student to write or verbally describe his experience is a unique activity that can help increase this communication skill.
- A foundation of facts is necessary for students to build knowledge. Sometimes students need to learn definitions. Instead of regular memorization, involving the sense of taste can help a student experience, and therefore more likely remember, a definition. For example, I taught my 9th grade students what an oxymoron is by having them eat a sour gummy worm. These candies mix the opposite flavors of sour and sweet, and my students were able to actually taste an oxymoron by eating one.

Spiritual-Metaphysical

I realize that, in stating such a controversial area is an intricate part of the teaching and learning process, I am subjecting myself to possible intellectual ridicule. Yet, isn't a goal of learning to free ourselves from the confines of our self-limiting intellectual bonds? With this in mind, I ask us each to step outside our circle of cerebral comfort and knowledge and consider the potential validity of the metaphysical as an authentic means of educating the whole person—an indispensable method of using all that is part of our human existence in the process of teaching and learning.

What is that which man calls *spiritual* or *metaphysical*? I have spent many years studying spirituality, the metaphysical realm, and what is often called the *sixth sense*. My studies have led me to ministers, medicine men, monks, and missionaries. This same research has directed me to study philosophy, Eastern religion, Western religion, and nature. In this journey, I have developed several definitions for spirituality, and I will share some of these in order to hopefully connect with something that engages each reader of this material. That which is spiritual can be defined in several ways:

- an inner, non-genetic sense of uniqueness, creativity, individuality, intuitiveness, and eternal existence;
- knowledge and skills based on an "inner sense" or "sixth sense" of things—a sense which may or may not be based on intellectual and physical reasoning powers;
- that which is beyond our physical level of understanding;
- the inward components of anything which holds life—often referred to as spirit or soul;
- the essence of all life—the spirit and soul—which is non-measurable, over which is formed a physical cloak of existence that is measurable—the mind and body;
- our meta-physical stability, our meta-matter; or
- the highest levels of each of our other senses.

(For more information on the subject of the spiritual, see Dr. Hilliard's book *Spirit-Ritual*.)

One of the reasons I see the need for the spiritual to be a sense added to education is because whether or not a teacher believes in that which is spiritual is irrelevant to the fact that the majority of individuals do—which means a majority of the students in our classes, and professors in our schools and universities, believe in the spiritual realm at some level of awareness. Over the past several years colleges and universities throughout the United States and other countries have conducted studies of spirituality among college students and professors, looking for answers and expectations about finding meaning in life, values, belief systems, character, and self-understanding.

One of the largest of these studies was conducted by the Higher Education Research Center at UCLA. The study notes that the majority of college students consider themselves spiritual, have a desire to know more about spirituality, and wish to become engaged in various spiritual activities. Students also expressed an expectation that the college experience should help them expand their personal spiritual journey and add to their spiritual growth. As for most professors, they also state that they are spiritual, but few feel prepared or comfortable discussing spiritual issues in the classroom (*Spirituality in Higher Education*).

Based on these findings, and drawing from questions utilized on a variety of other college spirituality surveys, in 2007 O'More College developed a spirituality questionnaire and conducted research with its student population of 220 students. Of those, 140 students, or 71% of that student population, participated. Below are some of the major findings.

O'More College of Design
Spirituality Questionnaire Findings

1. At O'More, 85% of the students consider themselves to be spiritual.
2. When asked if they were curious and in search of spiritual answers about life, 68% said yes.
3. When considering spirituality, there are several areas these students found to have the greatest significance:
   a. the development of values and virtues and seeing values and virtues modeled by their teachers: 92%. (Specific virtues noted were kindness, love, compassion, individual human value, humility, patience, peace, unselfishness, joy, and hope.)
   b. God: 79%
   c. finding meaning and purpose in life: 69%
   d. developing ethical and moral behavior and seeing ethical and moral behavior modeled: 66%
   e. developing meaningful and personal relationships: 66%
   f. the ability to provide meaningful service to others: 63%

g. creativity, intuition, inspiration: 62%

h. quality of life: 61%

i. nature: 54%

j. Christianity: 50%

k. religion: 50%

l. connection with the past: 37%

m. church: 30%

4. When asked which of the above should be a part of the *overall* college experience, the following responses were provided (in order as they were expressed):

   a. creativity, intuition, inspiration

   b. meaning and purpose in life

   c. ethical, moral behavior

   d. quality of life

   e. service to others

   f. virtues

   g. meaningful relationships

   h. connection with the past

5. Topics which students said college should address, but only through specialty courses:

   a. God

   b. Christianity

   c. religion

   d. church

6. When asked the type of spiritual activities and rituals students liked to participate in, they noted the following (in order as they were expressed):

   a. church

   b. nature and outdoor activities

   c. meditation/reflection activities

   d. prayer

   e. reading, studying the Bible

   f. creating meaningful relationships

   g. Christianity

   h. singing, music

   i. service projects

   j. worship

k. interaction with loved ones

l. mission work, cultural field trips

m. creative activities

n. learning about various religions, spiritual movements, and spiritual philosophies

7. When asked what their biggest turn-offs with spirituality have been they replied as follows (in order as they were expressed):

   a. closed-mindedness

   b. hypocrisy

   c. forced beliefs, rules

   d. pushy people

   e. organized religion

   f. judgmental, condemning behaviors

   g. unethical, immoral behavior within religion

What can we do with this information? First, we can determine how to best make the spiritual expectations and desires noted in number three and four above a part of the overall educational experience, while avoiding the negative concerns with many spiritual activities noted in number seven.

If the concept of teaching spirituality principles seems inappropriate for inclusion in a public education setting, I encourage the reader to re-apply the same concepts under another title: growth and development, service-oriented learning, ethical behavior, purpose-oriented teaching and learning, team-building or relationship-building, diversity training, or creativity and innovation studies.

Too often, "we separate head from heart. Result: minds that do not know how to feel and hearts that do not know how to think. We separate facts from feelings. Result: bloodless facts that make the world distant and remote" (Palmer 68). We cannot ignore the facts nor the feelings; we cannot ignore the impact of the important, deeper reasons behind teaching and learning. "Three important paths must be taken—intellectual, emotional, and spiritual—and none can be ignored. Reduce teaching to intellect, and it becomes a cold abstraction; reduce it to emotions, and it becomes narcissistic; reduce it to the spiritual, and it loses its anchor to the world. Intellect, emotion, and spirit depend on one another for wholeness...by *spiritual* I mean the diverse ways we answer the heart's longing to be connected with the largeness of life—a longing that animates love and work, especially the work called teaching" (Palmer 5). *Spiritual* is not a word we should fear, nor is it an educational concept we should overlook.

Words Associated with the Spiritual Senses

God	higher power	first cause
creator	creation	Christ
Buddha	Mohammed	Allah
Gandhi	Christianity	Judaism
Buddhism	Taoism	Confucianism
Hinduism	Native American	Islam
philosophy	baptism	angels
demons	supernatural	sacred
meta-cognitive	spirit	spirit-ritual
spirituality	soul	universal soul
religion	the unseen	enlightenment
mystery	tradition	mystic
sixth sense	the spiritual heart	transcend
authentic truth	a calling	a vocation
higher plane	faith	higher purpose
wholistic	spiritual energy	higher motives
confession	repentance	belief
spiritual journey	power	authority
deep emotions	kindness	healing
soul wounds	revelations	intuition
love	hate	virtue
joy	peace	honor

trust	forgiveness	morals
dreams	visions	insight
meta-emotions	ESP	wisdom
blessings	service	authentic bliss
mindfullness	inspiration	altruism
tranquility	finding meaning	hope
harmony		
epistemology—the study of knowledge		

Expressions of the Spiritual Sense

selfless	gentle	generous
holy	creative	unique
whole	patient	caring

Effective Teaching and Learning Methods for the Spiritual Sense

- Create a classroom environment that values work ethic.
- Maintain a level of peace and respect during group activities, even in debates.
- Use rules and procedures to construct a positive educational atmosphere.
- Utilize mistakes as a teaching tool for growth rather than punishment.
- Have students create life and career mission, vision, and purpose statements and a list of personal core values.
- Participate in various service projects relating to specific courses you teach.
- Use team building, group activities, and games.
- Allow for diverse exploration into a wide range of topics to help students find their passion.
- Involve students in self-reflection activities.
- Have students create things that offer specific meaning and inspire.
- Connect the present to the past and future with any topic.

- Encourage students in their strengths and direct them in understanding their weaknesses.
- Exhibit the virtues expected in students.
- Discuss and teach about ethical behavior in the workplace, in personal business, and in relationships.
- Use mentors, internships, and community projects.
- Provide trips to other countries, cultures, and states.
- Take any sense, or any activity, and determine a way to experience it in such a way to create a greater, higher, more beneficial meaning or purpose.

The intent with this topic is not to create a roadblock for intellectual thinkers, rather to examine the potential of a wholistic approach to teaching and learning by including the students' spirit and feelings in order to create whole learning. If spirituality involves an inner, non-genetic sense of uniqueness, creativity, individuality, intuitiveness, and eternal existence, students cannot release this inner creativity unless we as teachers provide spiritual teaching and our students are involved in spiritual learning.

An Experience in the Spiritual

Jessa Sexton

- Incorporating the spiritual sense in the classroom does not simply mean discussing religion and should never mean forcing a belief system on our students. The spiritual sense often relates to the emotions of our students. When I ask students to chart the six senses touched by their reading of a passage, I explain that the spiritual sense includes those elements of the reading that "touch" our feelings. Something in the writing may move us without referring specifically to a physical contact. If the students are emotionally involved with any reading, they are more likely to make memorable learning experiences.
- The spiritual sense can also refer to a higher level of the other five senses. Music can be experienced only physically, ears hearing the sounds while body feels the thumping of the bass. However, most of us are drawn to music because

of the spiritual or emotional reaction we have to the physical sounds. I know what kind of music I want to listen to
in order to inspire certain feelings. Certain songs make me
cry every time I hear them, either because of a memory that
arises or simply because the song itself creates a sadness
within me. Because of both its physical and spiritual level,
music often finds its way into my lesson plans.

The Multi-Sensory Oxford Experience

Jessa Sexton

Too many times when traveling, we fail to take in the experiences
of all our senses—leaving memories that sometimes only connect
to the visual photographs we took. Learning often occurs the same
way—leaving only snapshots of visual moments from a class in
our minds without recall of what was learned. To make sure I left
Oxford full of memories to share with anyone who would listen, or
pretend to, for years to come, I took in the town with every sense.
The following is an excerpt from my travel journal.

Sight is, of course, the first sense recognizably touched by the
grandness of Oxford. With my feeble American connections, I
have to say that the buildings of importance resemble old churches
back home. I actually have a hard time distinguishing the Oxford
college structures from churches. This is an interesting connection, though, considering the role of these spaces. A church is a
place set apart—often visually—as a place of worship. Likewise,
these college buildings and libraries are set apart for academics.
Visually they demand esteem and awe: feelings I wish for all learners in reference to their education.

Besides sight, there are particular sounds of Oxford. While vehi-
cle traffic is heavy in places, we have more often been warned to
keep our ears attuned for the whooshing of cyclists, who take little
account of pedestrians! Other sounds I will forever associate with
Oxford are the random (and often untimely, if you've no umbrella) pattering of rain and the soothing streaming of the fountain
outside my dorm window. Both of these remind me of learning:

the unexpected rain is a reminder of the times when learning opportunities pop up from nowhere—lessons outside the lesson plan that we can choose to ignore or let soak us through. The fountain is the Ever-Learner; as the water is ever in motion, so too may be our research and growing desire to discover.

My sense of touch is always activated, but rarely considered. I think of all the people I bump into on Cornmarket Street, people from all over the world. I think of grabbing a book of poems by my favorite poet from the library—and making sure to find the oldest, the most worn, the most loved. I think of the warmth of my sweater—and how glad I am to have brought it, just in case. The handshake of a new friend, the steadiness of the stair rail, the rocking of the train to Stratford, and the feel of the pen in my hand as I deliberately choose to hand-write (in honor of C.S. Lewis) instead of type. As a learner, I must take the time to reflect on my contact with the world around me, or that world will pass me by.

The tastes of Oxford are easy to identify. I simply think of David Woodfine, our high steward, as he delivers my evening meals—with the individual (and each delectable) separate courses: salad or soup; a plate of meat, potatoes, and vegetables; and the always-anticipated sweet. The formality of the meal is as the often lost formality in academia. I admit I enjoy my TV dinners as I view my crime programs, but how little I actually *taste* those meals. Here in Oxford, each plate, each course, sets up my palette for a taste *experience*. How we must strive as teachers to set apart our classroom experiences—instead of rushing from curriculum-demanded task to task—so that students can truly taste the splendour of learning.

Defining the smells of Oxford may seem more challenging, until I remember my first steps into the Tate Library of the Harris Manchester campus. The instant inhalation of centuries of knowledge filled my lungs with the aroma of all those books. A literature teacher (and lover of books young and old), I cannot hold a tattered hardcover without opening its pages and breathing in its scent. The smell of these books lining the shelves and walls of the

Tate Library reminds me of my connection as a learner to other learners. The other hands that held those books, eyes that read those pages, hearts that tasted their meaning, and the original minds that created that meaning (based on their own learning) are all in the breath of those books.

I am not alone as a teacher, as a learner. I am in a community of wealth in knowledge. May I open my senses and thrive in my learning.

Final Thoughts—Multi-Sensory Teaching and Learning

As we begin to *systematically* integrate the use of our senses (taking notes while listening to a speaker; seeing a texture, then touching it; observing a beautiful flower, then taking the time to experience its smell; tasting something, then researching the ingredients) our brain begins to *automatically* connect these senses so that we hear something and know how to best put what we hear into written form, we understand the texture of an object simply through observation, we know what a flower smells like just by sight, and we can identify a food's ingredients purely by taste.

By exposing our students' senses to our lessons, a connection of understanding and deeper levels of education can develop. These multi-sensory experiences can help us activate ways of teaching and learning we never before thought possible.

a street view of the main entrance to Harris Manchester College

Chapter 3
Hilliard Circle of
Teaching and Learning

Engaging students in high-level, critical
thinking and problem solving

The Circle

The ability to simply recall facts and provide definitions is lowest in the levels of learning, and while recall might accomplish the goal of assisting a school district in obtaining a good educational reputation, this ability does little to encourage individualized learning. Much more beneficial is the ability of students to analyze data, find answers, solve problems, and draw on their newfound information to obtain personal growth and fulfillment as well as benefit the society and culture in which they live.

Toward this end, I believe learning occurs in a circle. Within this circle I am identifying the sequencing as moving counterclockwise. For many cultures this counter movement signifies higher meaning (often designated as spiritual learning), and some studies of right and left cerebral hemispheres show more ability to engage the right hemisphere, and create better communication between the two hemispheres, by approaching things in a manner atypical from the norm. In this theory, learning begins at a low level, moves to higher learning, and finally comes full-circle, where the student has become the teacher. I use words that all end with "tion" indicating that something has, will, or needs to occur for learning to take place.

Stimulation: What can teachers use to initially engage the student?

The teacher enters the circle of learning by creating a stimulus, or by providing an opportunity for stimulation to occur, that produces a sense perception by the student. Herein teachers need to broaden their base of introduction. We rely far too heavily on visual and auditory stimulation, thereby often blinding and deafening our students to alternative sensory inspiration. This initial stimulant may be a story, a picture, a smell, a flavor or taste, various sounds or music, an activity, a joke, a question, a fantasy, a metaphor, or a poem—not a lecture. The first stimulation should formulate a "big picture" reaction: a broad view of the subject matter.

Sensation: What senses do teachers wish to stimulate?

A sensation can be described as the simple contact by one or more of the senses with a stimulant, or at a higher level as a reaction of the senses to stimulation. Here, I separate sense contact (sensation) from sense reaction. Sensation is the initial contact with the faculties or senses that receive impressions and then should respond to the stimuli: hearing, seeing, touching or moving, tasting, smelling, and the little understood metaphysical or spiritual sensation.

One might think of each of these senses as vibrational receptors. Sensory vibrations are emitted into the environment. Within the human mind and body are sensory receptors, uniquely designed counterparts that somehow puzzle-piece together with these vibratory waves and molecules to create sensory awareness and

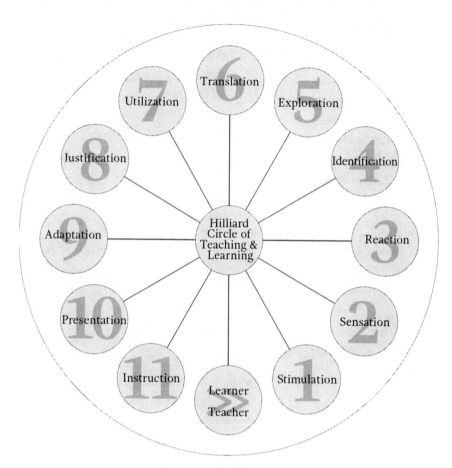

Exhibit
Hilliard Circle of Teaching and Learning Theory
Dr. K. Mark Hilliard
Copyright 2006

sensory perception. If there is little or no stimulation from the environment, little or no sensation occurs. Likewise, if there is continual, over-stimulation by the same stimulus, a loss of sensitivity to this stimulus occurs.

I believe that by involving all, or most, of the senses in the learning process, and by providing multiple and varied stimuli, there is better access to both the left and right cerebral hemispheres. In this bi-conditional atmosphere, whole learning can best take place.

Reaction: What reactions do teachers wish to receive from the student, and what reactions do we receive?

A student reacts to a stimulation of the senses based on the particular senses activated, hard-wired genetic factors, previous experience and knowledge, past relationship to the teacher, former experience with the stimulant utilized, and the environment for learning. Based on any of these factors the response may be positive, negative, or neutral. The response may also be a conscious, subconscious, or unconscious reaction based on stored memory.

Individualized learning materializes at this stage, because we each react differently to various stimulants based on our personal sensory interpretation. Sensitivity to culture, age, sex, individual interests, level of intelligence, level of ability, level of physical development, level of experience, and any other specific uniqueness of individual students must be considered in determining the stimulants to be used and the proposed reaction.

As teachers we want to interest, touch, move, engage, motivate, excite, direct, arouse, and even manipulate the reactions of our students' senses by using a variety of stimuli. The conventional lecture and handouts will not accomplish this type of positive reaction and will not engage students in higher learning.

Identification: What "initial" identification is made of what has been received at this point?

Initial identification is also typically based on past experience and knowledge, hard-wired genetic factors, or on a piece of new knowledge placed into the mind and labeled as so directed. This process centers on how well the sense reception or connection is made between the stimulus and the sense upon which an impression is made, and whether or not an additional sensory directive is made available. At this level of identification, we are talking about simple recollection of or introduction to labels, definitions, lists, names, places, dates, facts, statements, and records. This level involves rote identification or book knowledge. Complex identification and understanding requires an exploration into what has been identified.

Exploration: What experiences are provided for the student to explore and research—to become personally involved with the subject matter?

While the original stimulus may arouse only one or two of the senses, the stage of exploration should arouse and engage all, or most, of the senses. In order for students to sufficiently employ multiple sensations in the learning process, there must be excessive exploration, and the teacher must assume the responsibility for providing these opportunities, as well as training and guiding the students through the process. Few students know how to deliberately explore.

Sensory perception begins as we react to or identify a sensation, but true channeled perception does not occur until we begin to investigate and explore the sensation and add other organized sensations to the process.

True comprehension begins at this level, where the student gets personally involved by transferring what is held in the mind into form, through participation. The parts that make up the whole are not only identified, but are analyzed to determine how they make up the whole. Many methodologies used for teaching and learning through exploration are possible:

guided exploration	free exploration
field trips	travel experiences
research activities	personalized study
classroom discussions	question and answer activities
educational games	debates
scavenger hunts	meditative activities
experiments	investigative studies
practical, real-life experiences	

When we create opportunities for observation and encourage the skill of observation, simple and common elements of our every-day experiences at home, work, school, or play become wonderful occasions for sensory learning. The concept is to encourage students to search, investigate, reason, ponder, meditate upon, think through, experience, read intently, process, inspect, analyze, examine, question, probe, differentiate, compare, study, and to otherwise take an active, personalized role in their learning process. Students should both randomly and systematically explore the world.

Translation: What guidance is provided in helping a student personalize the material in a manner that relates to individual learning style and personal relevance?

Translation involves the student making a personal learning style connection between what is currently known and what is being learned, so that new learning may be applied to personal and new life situations. In this phase the material *becomes personally relevant* while interpreted, converted, or translated by the student. The material is *made uniquely appropriate, is applied to oneself, and produces practical value*. A student must be able to translate knowledge, skills training, symbols, and experiences into his or her internal, and often very individualized, process of cognition in order for practical meaning to occur.

This phase of teaching and learning is often overlooked by teachers and students, yet, without it, full comprehension cannot occur. Just as translation must occur when teaching and learning a foreign language, so must translation occur with any subject matter. In reality, many subjects remain "foreign" to our students because of the manner in which they are delivered. Until we as teachers learn to help our students translate learning, we might as well be speaking an actual foreign language.

Students need to be able to do many tasks in the translation phase:

apply	translate	convert
interpret	figure out	make practical
conclude	deduce	change
render	move from one place to another	
paraphrase	put into their own words	
transfer	create personal meaning	
transport	connect with meaning	

If students try to use a teaching without an understanding, not simply of the teaching itself but of the circumstance of the teaching—the original context and personal contextual application ramifications—they will fail in their ability to apply the teaching appropriately to a new situation. Teachers may use stories, analogies, dreams, fantasies, drawings, renderings, journals, diagrams, problem solving, games, and more to assist students in the translation of material.

Utilization: What opportunities can teachers provide the student to utilize newly learned knowledge and skills both in the classroom and out in the real world in which he or she must live and work?

Far too often we teach within the confines of the classroom, and our students have difficulty using their skills outside this setting. This difficulty is either a breakdown in the translation phase or a discomfort or disassociation with the new real-world surroundings. We need to expose students to real-life experiences and allow them to use their skills in this new environment—much like the concept of an apprenticeship.

Taking part in real projects with community agencies and internships are wonderful ways to incorporate the real world into classroom learning. At this stage of learning, the student utilizes what has been learned, and individualized, into a personal way of thinking. With this individualized thinking, the student creates something new:

an idea	an invention	a concept
a product	a formula	a theory
a law	a design	a piece of art
a poem	a book	a story
a building	a song	a piece of music
a prescription	an essay	a piece of advice
a thesis	an article of clothing	

The student produces something with personalized meaning and function that can also serve a greater purpose—something both functional and marketable.

Have students create answers to particular problems, ways to deal with specific needs, art or other creative projects, inventions, portfolios, journals, manuals, case studies, pieces of music, tests. To assist students in learning this creative skill, teachers should model learning by vividly demonstrating, having students help them in the process, and helping students in the process as needed. Finally, students should create or accomplish the task on their own.

Justification: What can teachers do to help a student critique and then justify personal work?

Higher learning has not taken place until a student can personally critique his or her own work and justify what has been created. Toward this end, the teacher must provide appropriate guidelines (criteria) in order for such a critique to take place. Left to their own, students seldom have the skills to justify their work. This personal critique can then be followed by a review and evaluation by peers, teachers, and professionals—in this order. The student must not only create, but must be able to explain and defend what has been created—what the creation is, why it is appropriate, and how it can be used.

Under the guidance of proper teaching, a student can become competent and secure in a personal understanding of his or her work and develop the ability to appropriately prove his or her case. Any significant idea or creation should be able to stand up to a logical process of review. If not, changes need to take place.

During the justification phase, the student should be able to perform several responsibilities:

justify	prove	support
defend	convince	evaluate
critique	review	assess
appraise	show value	support theory
check and re-check	cite supporting sources or evidence	

Teachers need to be encouraging during this process, and students must be taught to accept both positive and negative critique.

Adaptation: What should the student be able to do, under the guidance of the teacher, if the work cannot be justified?

If students cannot justify, they must be able to alter, adapt, modify, or make appropriate changes to better serve the intended purpose of the product or concept. They must learn how to address new information that has been discovered during the critiquing and justification process and incorporate this information into their plan. Students are seldom required to function at this high level, are often defensive of what they perceive as negative comments, and are frequently unaware of how to, or are unwilling to, make appropriate modifications.

Many actions can take place during the process of adaptation:

modifying	altering	changing
improving	adjusting	accommodating
renovating	editing	
harmonizing	making to meet standards	

re-doing	making something fit
remodeling	making something suitable
revising	making more appropriate

The teacher's role is to help students find their own mistakes and to explore ways to resolve—guided discovery.

Presentation: What opportunities can teachers provide for a student to formally present findings—to properly share what has been learned?

The presentation stage of learning should be addressed by the student with a passionate, interpersonal, professional expression of knowledge and skill. This is one of the highest levels of learning because this stage proves the student has the ability to express and share knowledge and skills as well as convince others that the product or concept is important. The student should be able to sell the audience on the concept, idea, or product being presented, making whatever is presented desirable and praised by those listening. Teachers should guide students through The Hilliard Circle of Teaching and Learning so they are prepared to adequately make a presentation with skill and confidence.

At the point of presentation, students should be able to articulate their new understanding through several abilities:

communicate	convey	share
demonstrate	explain in detail	portray
display	divulge	make known
express	execute	perform
enact	present	engage
enlighten	inspire	
create conscious awareness		

Do not ask students to make a formal presentation until they have been trained to do so through informal presentations to peers and teachers.

Instruction: What opportunities can teachers provide for a student to learn the art and science of teaching and learning?

I believe this level to be the highest level of all learning, in that students now become teachers. Not only can these students make a presentation, but they can teach others how to do what they can do, how to create what they can create. They can teach others how to stimulate, react, identify, explore, translate, utilize, justify, adapt, and present.

Methodologies used should allow students to tutor, demonstrate, student-teach, profess, instruct, oversee, serve as a guide, or mentor. For a student to reach this level he or she must gain an expertise, become competent in the subject matter, develop a mastery of appropriate knowledge and skills, and become adept in various teaching and learning styles—best directed by sensory perception.

Instruction can only be accomplished over a period of time, with effort, dedication, and strenuous thought and action. This level of learning requires an open mind toward learning and an expansion of one's circle of knowledge and beliefs. Within this level, the learner is required to reach outward and bring in those things that lead toward personal growth and development and then make use of that growth in helping others grow. At this point the student becomes the stimulus for someone else's learning.

(See *Chapter 7* for a lesson plan using the Circle.)

HCTL Level	Brief Explanation
Stimulation	Teacher stimulates students with **more of the senses** than simply sight and sound. This initial stimulant may be a story, a picture, a smell, a flavor or taste, various sounds or music, an activity, a joke, a question, a fantasy, a metaphor, or a poem. The first stimulation should formulate a **big picture** reaction—a broad view of the subject matter. Key Words: inspire, engage, big picture, motivate, interest
Sensation	Which **sense(s)** will the stimulation contact? The teacher is trying to help students become engaged in the learning by connecting with the students' senses and helping the students understand and notice which senses are being stimulated. Key Words: taste, touch, smell, sight, sound, emotional/spiritual
Reaction	The reaction questions how the teacher hopes the stimulation will **cause the students to respond**, and how the students actually respond based on past learning and experiences. Do the students enjoy the stimulation? Are the students intellectually aroused and asking questions? Key Words: negative, positive, neutral (the least desired response)
Identification	Students initially **categorize** based on first impressions and sensations. Key Words: label, define, list, name, date, record

Exploration	The students get personally involved by transferring what is held in the mind into form, through **participation**, while engaging and exploring all of the senses. Key Words: research, observe, search, investigate, question, compare, study, discuss
Translation	The students **personalize** the material, making **connections** between what is known and what is being learned by **applying** the learning to self, new situations, time, and the world. Key words: apply, interpret, paraphrase, deduce, conclude
Utilization	Students use skills and knowledge in the class and in the world (**real life**) through a personal **creation**. Key words: design projects, invent something, make a portfolio, produce an answer to a problem, create artwork
Justification	Students **critique** and **prove** the merit of their own work. Key words: defend, support, critique, review, assess
Adaptation	Students make **changes** based on discoveries in the justification phase. Key words: alter, modify, rewrite, revise, remodel, edit
Presentation	Students formally present findings to **share** with others what they have learned. Key words: communicate, share, demonstrate, explain, express, enlighten
Instruction	Students now become a teacher, **training** others **how** to do what they do and create what they create. Key words: guide, mentor, instruct, oversee, tutor

Final Thoughts—Hilliard Circle of Teaching and Learning

Jessa Sexton

In his book *Pedagogy of the Oppressed*, Paulo Freiere—called "perhaps the most significant educator in the world during the last half of the century" by Herbert Kohl (qtd. in Friere 16)—says, "Students, as they are increasingly posed with problems relating to themselves in the world and with the world, will feel increasingly challenged and obliged to respond to that challenge...Their response to the challenge evokes new challenges, followed by new understandings; and gradually the students come to regard themselves as committed" (81).

This method is in opposition to what Freiere calls the "anti-dialogical banking" education system in which teachers simply share "bits of information to be deposited in the student" (93). In Freiere's philosophies, "only dialogue, which requires critical thinking, is also capable of generating critical thinking" (92). His "banking concept" of education "encourage[s] passivity" (95) while "authentic education" happens when the teacher and the learner work together, with the teacher in a constant role as a learner as well (93).

Considered one of the greatest philosophers of all time, Aristotle said, "Those who know, do. Those that understand, teach." Our ability to instruct is verification of our education. Illinois-born writer and philosopher Elbert Hubbard writes, "The object of teaching a child is to enable him to get along without a teacher." I'd like to modify this idea only slightly: the object of teaching is to equip the learner with the knowledge, skills, abilities, and desire to become his own teacher.

The witty and sarcastic author Oscar Wilde writes, "Everybody who is incapable of learning has taken to teaching." When we lead our students to the highest level of learning through the dialogue of shared experiences; sensory connections; guided critical thinking, personalization, creation, and re-creation; and finally an understanding solid enough to share with others (this Hilliard Circle of Teaching and Learning)—we prove Oscar Wilde wrong; we demonstrate that teaching and learning are unequivocally concordant and that neither exists wholly without the other.

*Mark tries on an Oxford Tutor's robe
in the Senior Common Room.*

Chapter 4
Student-Centered Testing

Researching and applying alternative methodologies for teacher and student assessment within a specific populace or identified intelligence and based on measurable objectives for the mastery of skills and knowledge

Background Knowledge

With a knowledge and understanding of the students we are teaching, we can appropriately assess their progress, and we can make learning relevant to their real-life experiences. This initial analysis begins with an understanding of the community in which we teach, including the culture of the dominant and subdominant society. This understanding must continue into the classroom and to the individual learning styles of each student, something that can be learned only as both students and teachers share in the mutual experience of teaching and learning.

Purpose for Assessment

What are the general purposes for assessment?

- to judge students' current knowledge
- to determine whether or not teachers have been effective in disseminating knowledge
- to determine whether or not measurable objectives have been established and met—including the individual mastery of appropriate skills and knowledge
- to determine students' preparedness for continuing at a higher level of learning

But the greatest purpose for assessment *should* be to provide the learner with opportunities for improvement: learner-centered assessment. Many forms of testing seldom accomplish this objective because their goal is an end-result—*did the student "get it?"* Alternative assessment is designed to *assist the student in "getting it."* For this reason, alternative assessment methodologies should occur from the beginning of the teaching and learning process to the end, with guided direction throughout. Students have opportunities to correct projects, tests, theories, or concepts before they formally present them. Grading is in relation to progress en route of an intended end result, but the end result is secondary, the grade is secondary, to learning.

One might think that this format would lessen the ability to accomplish an intended end result, but in fact it fortifies an authentic end result because the genuine mastery of skills and knowledge becomes a natural by-product of the learner-centered assessment process. Students learn appropriate skills and knowledge to better themselves and to share their newly-acquired gifts and talents with others, rather than learning in order to pass a test.

Measurable outcomes *cannot* truly be measured by the giving of a *traditional test*, which might only demonstrate a student's ability, or lack of ability, to memorize. This does not negate the benefit of periodic traditional testing, but authentic skills and knowledge are only measured by a student's ability to translate and use the knowledge he has obtained and demonstrate the skills he has developed in a personal, functioning environment.

In this learner-centered process, certain criteria are set for each stage, and students typically move at various paces. This does not, however, imply that deadlines are not set and expectations not adhered to, but evaluation should always come back to meaningful purpose in the assessment procedures and guidance throughout.

The Learner-Centered Student Assessment Process

1. Create a list of skills and knowledge a student needs to master within a program, a department, a major, and for each course.
   - This should be assembled by academic leadership under the guidance of department heads and in conjunction with practicing professionals within a discipline, departmental advisory committees, and specific course faculty: such development should begin with a review of appropriate accreditation standards.
2. Ensure that teachers are knowledgeable and appropriately skilled in the subject matter, about the community in which they teach, and about the students who sit before them.
   - All potential teachers should be personally interviewed—preferably by more than one person.
   - Confirm resumes and educational credentials.
   - Carefully review past student evaluations and departmental evaluations.
   - Talk with previous department chairs or supervisors.
   - Ask for a teaching demonstration presented before an academic review committee.
   - Discuss the mission, vision, and educational philosophy of the school with all new teachers, and question them as to their educational philosophy.

- Conduct regular evaluations of teachers by their students and departmental academic staff; make sure the evaluation tool assesses skills and knowledge within the appropriate discipline, desire and ability of teacher to interact with students, and ability to teach, not just measures the popularity of the teacher.
- Within the first year of teaching, use teacher mentors to evaluate and encourage novice and new faculty.
- Encourage teachers to participate in community affairs, service projects, and public scholarship activities, and provide time off to be a part of community organizations.
- Share information with all new teachers that will make them familiar with the school system and the community.

3. Assure that teachers are apt and ready to teach with appropriate teaching and learning tools and demonstrate a love for teaching.
   - All teachers should be required to take continual teacher training every year.
   - Schools should create a means for formally recognizing and showing appreciation for those who excel in teaching and learning: reward good teaching.

4. Review the ability of students to think critically, solve problems, and find answers.
   - Appropriately directed and assessed research projects and exploration activities are wonderful as both learning and measuring tools.

5. Most assessment should be project-oriented, requiring students to translate and utilize both skills and knowledge through meaningful, practical application.
   - Take advantage of real-life experiences in the teaching and learning process as often as possible.

6. Provide opportunities for students to justify their work and, in so doing, find their own mistakes and make appropriate adaptations in order to correct these mistakes.

- As students informally present their assignments, they should have opportunities to correct projects, tests, theories, or concepts before they formally present them.

7. Provide opportunities for peer, professor, and professional reviews of each student's knowledge and skills as well as the student's ability to communicate, defend, and convince reviewers of his thinking or creations.
   - Provide multiple opportunities for students to present projects before these groups.

8. Require internships with specifically outlined and measurable outcomes.
   - On-the-job training, on-site instructing, and structured apprenticeships are great learning experiences.

9. Provide opportunities for students to offer their skills and talents to benefit their community and, when possible, the community at large.
   - In this effort, allow students to teach others what they have learned and how to do what they have learned.

Clear Expectations

Jessa Sexton

One of the most essential elements of any assessment—of any classroom—is clear expectations. When students would come to me expressing frustrations with other instructors, the issue often boiled down to the teacher failing to present clarity in what he desired from his students.

If you teach college, remember the significance of clarity in your syllabus about policies and procedures. Any other grade-level educator can create a similar document that sets up, at the very start of the class, details about how this relationship between teacher and student, student and material, and even teacher and parent will be handled. You may take a couple of years to refine your syllabus or class entry document to the point you feel it accurately prepares a student for your course, and don't be afraid of the trial and error that will come as you work on such refinement.

Many elements need to be clear to your students; a few such policies are listed below:

- late work
- missed assignments
- absences
- how best to get in touch with the teacher
- student email
- tardies
- student accommodations
- drop and add
- grade scale
- grading (point system, weighted grades, how the final grade is tallied)

A mission statement, ultimate class goals, and the expected mastery of skills and knowledge are good to include as well.

I knew a professor who took a letter grade deduction each day a paper was late. She rarely had a late assignment. For several of my writing classes, I gave ½ credit if the assignment was a week late and no credit after that. This system kept me from constantly grading late assignments, as I was busy enough keeping on top of current work. Some assignments received no credit if turned in late, unless the student had a doctor-approved reason. The key is making these procedures completely clear before any such assignment is ever turned in.

In my seven years teaching college level writing, reading, education, and communication classes, I found three specific terms that helped me become a professor with clear expectations: feedback, rubrics, and recaps.

Feedback

Jessa Sexton

A specific complaint I heard from students was that certain instructors gave little or rather late feedback. When we do this, we limit our students' ability to grow from their mistakes; we limit their chances to use those higher levels in The Hilliard Circle of adaptation and justification. If we don't give feedback on project number one until students are working on project number two or three, the student has probably moved on in thinking and could be continuing the same errors.

The *ADA Compliance 2013: Issues in Higher Education* guide suggests that educators should provide "feedback throughout an assignment process, instead of just at the end" (22). This recommendation is for students with disabilities but remains advantageous for every student. In doing so, we help the student identify and correct problems early on, giving the student a chance to turn in a final project or paper, or to take a test, feeling prepared and assured of his knowledge.

Feedback can include handwritten notes on an assignment, emails, comments inserted in the margins of a Word document, and observations during class time—all delivered in a *timely* manner. I've had students turn in final drafts or deliver final speeches that carried the same mistakes as an earlier draft. When their grades suffered, I was able to remind that student of the feedback that was clearly provided early enough for changes to occur. I cannot make my students adapt their work, but if I have told them the necessity of doing so, their final grade is dependent on their heeding such warning.

Rubrics

Jessa Sexton

Another "such warning" I give my students—making my expectations on a particular assignment clear from the beginning—is a rubric, given to them as the project is dispensed. My rubrics have ranged from brief to incredibly detailed, depending on the amount of clarity I feel the assignment needs. On each rubric, I assign point values to each defined expectation. When I hand out rubrics, I review them verbally with my students; I ask if they have questions; I tell them to use the rubric as they work on the assignment; and I tell them to turn that same rubric back in with the assignment.

When I was in college, my own professors encouraged me to ask other teachers or search online when starting a new rubric. Creating one can sometimes take a lot of time, and there is no need to completely re-invent the wheel, they explained. The more I taught, the more I was able to open up an old rubric and adapt it for a new assignment, but those first couple of years were tough. (I have included some sample rubrics in *Chapter 7*.)

One thing that helped me in creating rubrics was doing each assignment on my own. I wrote every essay and research assignment; I crafted each speech project. In doing so, my expectations became clear—to myself. Only then could I define these expectations to my students. Though extra work in the beginning, this process connected me to my students both by guiding my communication with them in the project and helping my understanding, ahead of time, of the difficulties they might encounter along the way. Also, I had a good stack of examples I could provide students when necessary.

The final comment I would like to make about the value of rubrics is this: when I used this assessment tool, I easily stood firm in my grading process, both for me and for my students. I couldn't favor a student; the rubric guided my grading. When I incorporated this tool into my classroom, the grade-complaints dwindled away. Students knew what I expected, and they saw my evaluation process clearly.

Recaps

Jessa Sexton

My schedules had the topic of the day and anything due that class period cleanly labeled, but sometimes an inspiration for a special class activity would come to me the night before. That point combined with the fatigue of hearing questions whose answers I know I had covered in class brought me to realize the importance of recaps.

I want to make a special note immediately: while I believe every teacher should employ some level of recapitulation, I also believe you have to decide for yourself at what level this would constitute as "hand holding." Perhaps you feel the need to recap more information for a particular course than for another. In any case, this idea deserves your deliberation.

I've used various means of delivering recaps, and I have heard of various others:

- posting online (for students and even parents, if applicable) the day's assignments and activities (with attachments of any handouts);
- emailing all students after class (with attachments of any handouts);
- using *Educreation.com* to create recap lectures with visuals;
- ending each class with a brief overview;
- having students summarize the main points of class before exiting (perhaps in a written format);
- beginning the next class with an overview of the previous one; or
- having students lead the next class with an overview of the previous one.

Whatever your method, I do suggest giving students a means of uploading certain handouts on their own, especially rubrics, the syllabus, or other papers you may or may not want to print and definitely don't want to hear students groan about losing.

Shelley Manns, a professor and the Assistant Director for Learning Support at Columbia State Community College, shared the *Educreation.com* tip with me. Manns makes a short recap video after class to highlight what was said, and sometimes to bring up new points she thought of after-the-fact. She emails all her students these videos and tells them to save each one. Her classes meet in a computer lab, and she encourages her students to bring earbuds so that, if they ask her about a point she already covered in class, she can tell them to pull up that video as a reminder. If they have further questions on the topic after reviewing that video, she is glad to answer these new problems without repeating herself constantly.

Feedback, rubrics, and recaps: all three hinge on the idea of a valued line of communication between the teacher and the student on their journey, together, of learning. Without a set of expectations clearly conveyed, students will grow frustrated, feel undervalued, and ultimately fail to work through the learning process. However we decide to go about it, we educators must define our desires and demands.

I can remember getting a B on a paper only because it ran one line longer than the required two pages. This grade was the teaching-moment for me in this professor's expectations, but it was a painful one. Two pages meant *two pages*. I remember a high school teacher handing me back a draft of my final paper again and again, telling me it wasn't right. He finally explained the expectation I failed to meet: he wanted better transitions. In both of these instances, I could have met these desires immediately, had I clearly known them. I tell my students that the first couple of assignments and tests are often the learning experience of figuring out what a professor wants—but if we, as professors, can think back to this frustrating process, maybe we will do a better job of communicating, *at the onset*, who we are, what we want, and how a student can flourish in our class—and therefore in his learning.

Teaching through Tutorials:
The Oxford Experience

Jessa Sexton

Learning more about the Oxford tutorial system has helped me analyze my teaching style and rethink just how well I use the time my students invest in my class each semester. When talking with Lesley Smith, a Senior Tutor of Harris Manchester College of the University of Oxford, I learned that students generally take two tutorial courses each semester. Each course involves meeting with a tutor and another student one hour each week for the eight-week semester.

During the time between meetings, the student will take on the task of sifting through "more reading material than one can actually handle," as Smith describes it, with the goal of learning how to process large amounts of information and figure out what has value. (Each week will have its own topic, and the readings coordinate.) Whatever the student finds valuable in his reading will be considered and processed as he writes a weekly paper. Lesley Smith explains that the paper is generally 1,500 words, though she once had a student who wrote 4,000 nearly every time! Students are encouraged to connect their thoughts for each paper with previous learning relatable to the week's topic as well. These papers not only help students learn priorities and connections, they also teach students how to structure their ideas into a readable, relatable format.

The one-hour meetings of the student, his peer, and his tutor are a time in which Smith says "real conversation on the topic" is the ultimate aim. Generally, the students move away from what was written in their papers as they begin to think beyond their initial impressions on the subject and form new ideas—ideas that cannot be created by solitary reading and writing, ideas created by questioning and by turning feelings about the topic into dialogue and explanations.

I think any educator can see the worth of this instructive system. Communication and the ability to pick out important facts from a large amount of material are two talents required for success in the modern world. Also, for any teacher who has tried to make sense of a student's essay, you know the value of a student learning how to structure and outline. Many times I've wondered if a student typed up his ideas, cut them all up, and dropped them, helter skelter, onto a piece of paper while feeling the triumph of having completed his final essay for my class.

So how can I achieve a bit of the tutorial benefits in my own classroom? First of all, I can take the time to meet with my students in small groups. In the college setting, I will have a day or two in our semester set aside for students to sign up for time slots instead of coming to the entire meeting time. I notice that groups of three are better than four; with four students one can still hide behind the others. Our shorter small group meetings always get more done for the individual students then a full lecture class can.

If you do not teach at the college level, you can still find ways to set up similar moments. I remember that when I taught 9th grade English, there were days I let them have private reading time. This would be a perfect moment for you to call out small groups for discussions on certain topics. Another method is making yourself present during small group activities. My personal temptation was to use small group times as a chance to catch up on my grading, but not all groups are mature enough to make worthwhile development on their own. Moving around the room, asking questions here and pushing progress there, will be of benefit to your students.

These are only two suggestions on how you can incorporate some of the Oxford tradition for excellence in education into your own classroom. I challenge you to see the value in giving some of your academic self in a small group setting and pondering how you can instill the ability of your students to learn discernment and communication. These skills will vault them into new scholastic heights.

As I noted in my personal research into the tutorial approach to teaching and learning, most of the educational objectives of the tutorial system are obvious within the methodology itself:

- expansive personal research;
- independent or self-determined thinking;
- the building of confidence as a student must defend a given topic; and
- the building of organizational and writing skills.

I find that students within the tutorial system are personally stimulated to *find* material on a given topic, to *read* and *evaluate* its relevance, to *translate* this material into their ways of thinking, to *write* an adequate paper addressing the topic, and then to *present and defend* the material before a small group of students and a tutor—who are likely as knowledgeable, or more knowledgeable, than the student on the topic of discussion. These moments create a wonderful opportunity for intellectual discourse.

The various levels of learning required for tutorial sessions automatically support my theory that the more senses we involve in the teaching and learning process, the more we learn. The tutorial system is a multi-sensory approach to teaching that allows the tutor to easily adjust his or her teaching style to each individual student, a difficult task in a regular lecture-style class. Each student is able to learn from the teaching and learning styles of the tutor and other students in each session. The tutorial system requires each student to see, hear, touch, and, in essence if not in reality, to smell and taste the topic of study. Tutorials require each student to become emotionally involved with the subject matter at hand, something we seldom accomplish in the lecture format of teaching (though *Chapter 6* discusses methods to improve our lectures).

In *Oxford Magazine*, Oxford Tutor Abdul Raufu Mustapha describes benefits of the tutorial system:

- the idea of "starting where the student is, and building on strengths and interests" (21);
- the ability to quickly know each student's strengths and weaknesses;
- the benefit of a less formal methodology for sharing teacher "insights and observations" (21);
- the chance for students to make mistakes and grow in the learning process, rather than being punished without the opportunity to correct the mistakes;
- the individual attention of this format of teaching and learning; and
- the opportunity for tutors to help their students "master the big ideas, and then to take a more rounded and critical view of the actual material of the curriculum" (22).

Mustapha believes that the tutorial system of teaching and learning far exceeds any other teaching method for reaching the inner-depths of any topic. The major goal of tutorials is to improve the student's skills, knowledge, and ability to intellectually argue a given topic.

In the magazine, another Oxford Tutor, Robin Briggs, explains the best tutorial system circumstances (20):

- Students taught through the tutorial system will typically do very well in their learning process as long as they feel the tutor is showing a true interest in them and is valuing the work created and presented by each student—something the structuring of the tutorial system strongly supports.
- Tutorial teaching works best with three students, which seems to compel each student to come to each session prepared to discuss. Where there are more than three students, some are likely to be slack in their preparation.

Oxford Tutor Todd Huffman expresses the need for our teaching and tutorial methods to assist students in "unlearning a great deal of natural conditioning that we are born to" (20). This requires the use of practicing professionals who are themselves active or who have been recently active in research for their given fields. When the tutors are active professionals, they have the skills and knowledge to address current problems and misconceptions students will face in their personal research. Huffman supports assessment of teachers and tutors, but believes colleagues and students are the best source for this assessment.

While I believe the tutorial approach to teaching and learning to be a superb format for reaching our students, I also understand the limitations imposed on colleges by our United States structure of required clock hours in the classroom for each hour of credit offered the student. I do, however, believe that we also place an abundance of self-imposed limits on our approaches to teaching and learning based on either our lack of willingness to expand our teaching role into more of a tutorial formula, or our lack of knowledge of how to follow such an approach. Below, I provide several practical approaches to using the Oxford tutorial system within the United States school structure:

- The university system has a tendency to "grow large." Sometimes "grow smart" is better. Opening more sections of a given course and keeping the teacher-student ratio low allows teachers the ability to set up individual meetings with each student, whereas large classes make this a timing impossibility.
- Make a point to meet with each student at least once outside the regular classroom situation during a semester, or set up times to meet with small groups of students during or after regular class sessions.
- Give students a well-defined outline of books and materials on a topic, along with a well-defined list of intellectually meaningful and thought-provoking questions for which they must explore and create responses. Have only a small number of students make presentations on any given day, followed by class discussion. (With more than three or four presentations on a given day, students tend to disengage at some point in the process.)
- Make use of e-mail to get to know students: create e-tutorial sessions, e-discussion groups, e-assignments, and

e-assessments. While I strongly believe that personal meetings with students are extremely important, I have also come to believe that some students excel in the less personal world of technology. By knowing each student, you will better know how to approach his or her learning comfort zone.

Final Thoughts— Student-Centered Testing

Some of the most meaningful alternative assessment methodologies include things students can do other than take tests:

- journaling of daily activities (usually presented in the students' own words or styles);
- charting, mapping, circling, trailing of learned information;
- creating a test following a specific educational format and presenting to the class;
- translating and using information by applying learning to their personal lives through self-application questioning directed by the teacher, or self-application journaling;
- working up sketches, drawings, or other creative expressions of learned material;
- creating portfolios, display boards, or models;
- researching and presenting on specific topics;
- creating detailed case studies of special subject matter;
- employing sensory awareness activities—finding ways to relate any of the senses to a subject;
- creating a full spectrum of projects including investigative studies, creative art and design assignments, experiments, individual and group assessment of others' works, books, projects;
- developing new inventions, concepts, or ideas; and
- participating in well-organized internships and apprenticeships.

When you do try out a new assessment or teaching method, collecting feedback from students can be a helpful practice. One "well-known classroom assessment technique," according to Penn

State Professor Emeritus of Teaching and Learning Maryellen Weimer, is "called the 'minute-paper,' in which students use the last few minutes of a class to quickly identify content that they do and don't understand and about which they'd like to learn more" (57). These quick comments give students who wouldn't speak up in class a chance to ask questions, allow all students to summarize what they learned and what they didn't quiet understand, and provide the educator with reactions to how the lesson was received. Such knowledge can guide future assessment decisions.

"Competent practice is knowing how to adapt a technique, strategy, or policy so it fits the content, context, and instructor" (Weimer 58). When we implement a new evaluation process, we have to think ahead to how we can make it work best with our students and also think *behind*, so to speak—after the assessment has occurred—on how effectively it represented our students' learning.

This field of alternative assessment is limitless in the number of ideas a teacher can apply to guiding and evaluating students. And the best quality of alternative assessment is that these forms of evaluation are individually created to meet each specific need and are flexible in the way they can be used with individual students.

*a view from right outside Mark and Jessa's dorm
at Harris Manchester College*

Chapter 5
Classroom Environmentalists
The construction of a unique physical and psychological campus and classroom environment

The Educational Ecosystem

We must produce a campus and classroom environment that, along with the other components of the *Educational Wellness* philosophy, creates an educational ecosystem: a community of administrators, teachers, parents, students, and others whose skills, intellects, experiences, and dispositions create psychocenosis—a mingling and sharing of minds with common interconnected goals. Consideration is also due to a physical environment of buildings, facilities, and grounds that inspire minds and spirits toward creative thinking. Together, these elements create an overall environment conducive to whole teaching and learning.

Administrators, teachers, and community leaders must be sensitive to this teaching and learning atmosphere. If the teaching environment is not conducive to the intended result of learning, the environment must be changed. If the environment cannot be changed, a move to a better environment must be sought. And if a move cannot be accomplished immediately, teachers must be flexible and adapt their teaching accordingly. Just as undesired and displeasing sensory exposure can provide immense distraction, a positive, desired environment can set the stage for successful teaching opportunities.

The Sacred Learning Space

The overall intent is to create a sacred learning space, a space *set apart* for higher, creative learning. Such a place can be specifically described as being

- free of clutter;
- organized with the ready availability of appropriate teaching tools (audiovisual equipment, drawing boards, desks, books, visuals);
- representative of the students being taught—age appropriate with student work on the walls;
- suitable in size for the number of students within the room; and
- designed with appropriate color psychology for the intended audience and subject matter. (Changing paint colors is one of the more effective and least expensive ways to change the physical environment.)

Also, such a space should have particular natural necessities:

- appropriate and adequate lighting, including some natural lighting;
- adequate and fresh air flow;
- moderate, controlled heating and cooling;
- representations of life and energy such as plants, animals, natural objects, or photographs or paintings of nature; and
- a feeling of safety and comfort.

Students tend to adapt to whatever space is provided, but as they adapt their creative and critical thinking skills may also adapt, which may be good or bad depending on the type of environment.

Emotional Setting

Jessa Sexton

"Learners need to adopt attitudes and strategies that pay off in terms of low anxiety, high motivation, and ultimately in the ability to convey information and communicate ideas and feelings" while teachers need to "provide students with a learner-centered, low-anxiety classroom environment" (Young 426). Though Dolly Jesusita Young's quote is in reference to language learners, this method applies to any student.

The physical elements of a classroom are only part of what we must consider as we create what Mark described as a sacred space for learning. Sometimes much of the physical (paint color, furniture, view, even temperature) is out of our hands as educators. When I taught 9th grade English, I placed student art over the bland cinderblocks, but I had no control over the chairs or desks. I've taught in rooms that had only two temperatures possible: freezer or furnace.

Yet with those elements against me, I still had the ability to lead the emotional environment, and this element cannot be overlooked as we prepare to enter the circle of teaching and learning with our students.

"Curriculum consists not just of contents and outcomes...it also consists of places, typically classrooms, where the business of learning is transacted and it is on the quality of life lived in classrooms that many of the things we hope from education depend—concern for community, concern for others, commitment to the task in hand" (Fraser foreword). Barry J. Fraser's research should help educators in "understanding classroom environment as a component of curriculum" (forward). His book provides "compelling evidence" that shows "that having constructive classroom environments is an intrinsically valuable goal of schooling...that the classroom environment is such a potent determinant of student outcomes that it should not be ignored by those wishing to improve the effectiveness of schools" (1).

What constitutes the "constructive classroom environment" Fraser says is intrinsic to improving education?

"Most learning is not the result of instructions. It is rather the result of unhampered participation in a meaningful setting" (Illich). And this meaningful setting includes the physical surrounds and also the atmosphere: "the space should be hospitable and 'charged,'" giving students a feeling of safety while still encouraging risk taking (Palmer 78). In that latter quote, Parker Palmer uses excellent words that clearly define the balance needed in an effective classroom environment: a space both welcoming and stimulating; a space that feels safe but is also challenging.

How can we create such a well-rounded (wholistic) setting?

I have worked my entire scholastic career with the mindset that goals and standards can be set high when students are motivated through encouragement of accomplishment, pushing students to desire success in areas they perhaps once thought beyond them as they are shown the importance of learning and the achievability possible. For me, the two words that are key to defining my responsibility in this academic area are *encouragement* and *enthusiasm*. When students see our passion, when they realize we believe they can succeed and are readily available to help them do so, when they are guided past a fear of failure into an atmosphere that is "hospitable" and also "charged," safe and challenging—they have entered a suitable environment set apart for the revered undertaking of teaching and learning.

The Classroom Environmentalist: The Oxford Experience

The whole environment of the Colleges of the University of Oxford provides multi-sensory inspiration that seems to permeate everything about the Oxford experience. You walk into any of the multi-college campuses already engaged and ready to learn. In my words it is an "academic nirvana." In the words of one of our younger members, it is "so cool." But we both, though perhaps through different translations, saw and felt very similar emotions.

And in actuality, we both probably came to Oxford with certain preconceived images of academic nirvana and coolness already in our psyche, which were fortunately revealed to be real. Oxford brought our images, as prophetically anticipated, to true light.

In our own colleges and schools, we create images as well—preconceived and real images. We must strive to build powerful, engaging, yet realistic images and, even more so, make certain our images shine true under the light of inspection. A preconceived image that fails to hold true, or a poor image, keeps a campus and classroom environment from being conducive to whole teaching and learning.

The Oxford atmospheric environment is created in large part by the attention to detail in everything from the architectural design of the buildings to the academic design of the curriculum and the teaching and assessment methodologies. But I feel a major strength of the Oxford environmental experience is that each college, and even each unit within a college, though in many ways separate entities from the overall University, offers a rigorous effort to make everyone a joint-member of the whole. Everyone who becomes a part of the University of Oxford system, or becomes attached to any college within, becomes a member, in some way, of the whole. Everyone feels, and in actuality is, a part—everyone becomes a *member* of the University of Oxford.

Our students and our teachers need to feel a part of the unit of a classroom, of a department, and of the school or university as a whole. As fellow members the faculty, staff, students, and others associated with a school can better create a symbiotic relationship—a relationship developed out of a feeling of mutual respect and anticipated integrity. The actual titles of something such as student members, supporting members (active parents and financial supporters), and honorary members, as well as our typical informal title as faculty members, is a concept that American schools and colleges would do well to consider as a way to establish unity.

The doorways, the outdoor gardens, and the pathways of our colleges all lead somewhere, and inquisitive minds and legs are made to wander their course. These spaces are an open invitation to learn—the environment shouts it out loud, or perhaps whispers privately to each who walks the grounds. An environment of beauty requests an audience of participants. We do much too little in most of our schools to appeal to this inner, sensual desire to resond to outer aesthetic quality. Students, as well as the faculty and staff of a school, are greatly affected by their surroundings. Are the surroundings of your establishment encouraging and engaging all to learn?

The Classroom Environmentalists— Final Thoughts

What is the purpose for making appropriate changes to the psychological and physiological school environment? The attitude of students and teachers about coming to school, learning, creating, and even taking tests will change—a change that now allows for whole teaching and learning to occur.

Mark in front of Duke Humphrey's
Reading Room of the Bodleian Library

Chapter 6
The Art of the Lecture

Part One

Jessa R. Sexton

The Old Lecture

Most of my educational approaches from the professor side of the classroom include a myriad of audio-visuals. I incorporate the PowerPoint, food object lessons, and activities galore. But lately both Mark and I have been pondering the Art of the Lecture.

My literature college professors pretty much always stood in front of their classrooms for hours with yellowed notes and endless knowledge. They spoke about what they knew, and I relished taking it all in. I didn't feel cheated without the PowerPoint. I didn't long for rousing classroom activities. And yet, our students often complain to us about such lecture methods today.

I get lost in my thoughts and cannot pay attention.
Her voice tends to drone on, and I lose concentration.
I don't feel involved.

These are just some of their comments. And I know I cannot say to them, "But I loved that type of classroom environment back in my day" (*my day* getting further back in time each passing year that I teach), because I *love* academia, and the old lecture style can be enthralling rather than daunting to me.

When Technology Fails

Last semester I came to a particular class full of great PowerPoint presentations, with video clips and sound bites. The computer failed me. Four weeks in a row. By the time everything was working again, that excellent introduction to class presentation would have been out of place to share. Sometimes "the best-laid schemes o mice an men gang oft agley" (Burns ll. 39-40).

We've discussed in this book multiple ways to engage your students, but the past year we've wondered: how can you be engaging if all you have is your body and a white board? We decided to consider what *Old School* really means. Can you teach an old lecture new tricks? Can we bring back the art of the lecture, without *bells and whistles*, so to speak, but still with a lot of *pomp and circumstance*?

These Five Things

Later in the chapter, Mark writes about subject matter, audience, environment, and the speaker. In my section, I want to examine some areas I've been exploring in my classroom over the past year: discussion, note-taking, your body, illustrations, and storytelling.

1. Discussions

The old lecture style rests on a one-directional conversation: the professor speaks; the students listen. Moments exist in the classroom when this method can thrive, and Mark's section will, in part, cover how to make those moments a success.

However, one of those complaints I listed earlier (*I don't feel involved.*) can be erased by incorporating discussion throughout the lecture.

Oh no. I said the teacher's d-word. *Discussion? Seriously? You must have never had that moment of excruciating silence that fills every crevice of the classroom after you ask a question no one answers.*
Yes, I have. And I've been on the other side. I've been the student who cannot handle that silence and feels an intensive pressure to answer—to say anything even halfway intelligent sounding just to make it stop.

Don't worry. I have learned a few tricks to keep those painful pedagogical moments from happening.

Let them prepare an answer.

If you don't want the silence, and you don't want halfway intelligent answers (or simple bunk answers) a student makes in an effort to fill the void, give your students time to prepare for what you will be asking. Sometimes I make a list of the questions I want to ask throughout the lecture. This takes some forethought, but it also helps me prepare. As I am a literature professor, I may ask about a character's motivation, a symbol's hidden meaning, an underlying theme. These are not easy questions to answer on the fly, even if you've read the assignment thoroughly. If I want thoughtful answers that can lead to even more class discussion, I shouldn't expect that to happen instantaneously after the question comes from my mouth.

Before I even begin the lecture, I will put students in groups. Each group has a couple of the questions I will want answered throughout the lecture. They have to come up with *source-supported* answers. In other words, whatever they write down needs to have references back to the text. This method works for any subject matter and makes the students accountable for their opinions.

Do you ever feel rushed at the start of class? Perhaps you walk around to check the previous night's homework, or you are taking attendance, or you are drinking bottled water because the walk up three flights of stairs winded you. In any case, you can become fully present and ready for class to begin as the students are busily preparing thoughtful, researched answers.

No more blank stares. No more, *Can you repeat the question?* from a student who spaced out or wants one more second to stall. When you ask, you will receive. And what you receive will have depth and direction.

Let them consider after.

I had a student tell me she enjoys a similar atmosphere *after* a portion of the lecture. She said she likes to break a lecture up by having group time to discuss and answer professor-provided questions in the middle. Maybe you've finished talking about one short story and are about to move on to the next. Pause. Put students in groups. Give each group a topic, a character, an important moment in the story—or whatever works with your subject. Reconvene, and let everyone share, or go around and let each group speak just to you, as you give immediate feedback and perhaps guide with another idea to consider and continue discussing. I've even had students illustrate their answers, with page references to the text to support the details they draw.

It's still a lecture, but it's broken into pieces—with time to reflect on all the beautiful knowledge you just imparted. Let students know this group discussion break will happen; tell them to take notes to guide their group time. This forewarning will help them in a couple of ways: they will see a proverbial light at the end of the lecture tunnel that may help them focus better as you speak; the encouragement to take notes will engage them; knowing they will have to talk about what you are talking about gives them an extra reason to pay attention.

When the group discussion is complete, take a break or reunite and move on to the next topic of the lecture. They have physically and mentally moved around the room, and they will be better participants in what is to come.

Give them more directive homework.

As I am writing this, I am in the middle of a summer literature course on Ernest Hemingway. The first day of class, I wrote some key words on the board: food and wine, women, honor, simplicity and sparseness, and internal thoughts. The class has seven students. I instructed each student to pick a topic, and no topic could be picked by more than two students. I told the students that, as they journaled, they could write down anything that interested them in the readings, but I wanted them to focus on their topic and its presence in Hemingway's work.

This idea gives their journal direction, but it also helps in our classroom discussions. Certain students will talk throughout the class with ease, but a few are naturally quieter. I know each student's topic, so the quiet ones cannot escape me. However, because I know each student's topic, I know I will not embarrass or single out anyone uncomfortably. When the student who is reading up on women hasn't said anything in a while, I can ask him a *pointed question* that I know he will have an answer for (as long as he has done his reading).

Also, if I were in one of those painful classes full of quiet students who just won't share, I would have a way to ask any student a direct question she should have a prepared answer for. We become accountable to each other. I, the professor, will get to know you, the student, better through the specific study you picked. You, the student, will need to prepare and do your reading assignment because you *will* be called on.

Also, the topics I wrote on the board were *my picks*: things I knew were present in Hemingway's writings. Therefore 1) I have some background knowledge about each topic, and 2) I know the student will find plenty to journal about. But, by letting students select from my list, they get a level of ownership that makes them feel more involved in their study and in my lectures.

2. Note-taking

When I entered college, the first shock to my academic system was how ill-prepared I was to take notes, and, therefore, to study. I cannot clearly remember what I did in high school to prepare for a test. I vaguely remember pouring over handouts for chemistry and Shakespeare, but nothing more.

Some students aren't taught the art of note taking, or, if they are, they are forced to follow one "proven technique" that may or may not connect to how they actually learn. Your students' abilities to take notes will vastly affect the effectiveness of your lectures.

Taking a couple of hours to talk about journaling and note-taking wouldn't be a waste of your class time. Depending on the course, you could offer different note-taking mini-lessons at the start of each class, letting students experiment with options until they find what works best for them.

Personally, I found that hand writing my notes, and then typing them up later, was the best way for me to take in the information during class and later organize and add my own thoughts. I know Mark likes to translate as he takes notes, but my mind doesn't always work that quickly. Often I write down things *word for word* as I hear them, adding questions or comments of my own under or on side margins if there is time, and save my reflections and deeper connections for later.

Some note-taking trials you may suggest or try out with your students could include the following:

- first try quoting;
- try another time jotting down general ideas;
- try once again writing main topics with blanks underneath to fill in throughout the lecture; and
- try a last time translating—writing out how the different pieces of the lecture connect in your mind or to other things you know.

Also have students play around with their medium. Some students must hand write: with a pencil, or a pen, or multiple color pens so as to organize and separate as they go. Others prefer to type (though you have to keep your eye on them or have some method of accountability so that they don't play around on the internet the entire time).

If you want to encourage your students to take notes, because you believe in the value of this physical connection with the lecture, you can follow Parker J. Palmer's method: "Because my students did not know whether I would gather and grade their notes...or ask them to use their notes for personal reference in small groups...all of them made notes, 'just in case'" (Palmer 82).

A great lecture leaves pieces of itself behind—as students linger on ideas, question a new topic, remember excellent points—and note-taking is essential for many students in recalling and reflecting; it is a well-valued skill that is given too little time of exploration. If you can help your students discover their best note-taking methods, they should find more clarity and focus, less frustration and boredom.

3. Your body

Mark later discusses one element of the body specifically important to artful lectures: the voice. Here, I want to talk about using some physicality in your presentations. "Social learning theorists contend that **attention** is a critical factor in learning" (Ormond np), and using your body as a tool you always have on you is an excellent way to capture and keep the attention of your students.

When studying *Hamlet*, I like to show my students different clips of the famous "to be or not to be" speech, interpreted by several different actors. Afterwards, we talk about what we did and didn't like about the performance. Most students enjoy Mel Gibson's performance because he conveys well the emotion of the words. An actor's vocal and physical performance of Shakespeare makes all of the difference. The Bard's vocabulary is one of the first comprehension problem areas for readers: but Shakespeare's work was, most of all, meant to be seen in performance.

Sometimes whatever you are talking about needs the emotional connection of your voice and body. Explaining this idea to my speech students, I once climbed up on a desk to recite Shakespeare's "Shall I Compare Thee to a Summer's Day" from memory. The repositioning of my body (to such a completely different location such as *up on a desk*) mixed with my ability to cite poetry from memory (a lost art form these days) combined to make the delivery of material more understandable and memorable.

Maybe climbing up on a desk makes you nervous. Many other physical considerations can be made, if this one doesn't seem to fit your personality.

- Make sure you don't stand in the same spot the entire class period.
  - Move around the room—not in a frantic or frenetic fashion, but in a controlled way.
  - Know your topic well enough to step away from the podium! (Yet even moving with notes in hand is still better than standing in one spot for the class's duration.)
  - Repositioning yourself helps your students pay attention, and helps you make eye contact with students you may not otherwise see from only one vantage point.
- Which brings me to this important tip: make eye contact with each of your students.
  - They will feel more involved if you give them this acknowledgement of their presence.
- If what you are talking about could better be illustrated by some sort of movement—*make that movement* (or have students make that movement).
  - Have your body become involved in your lecture. You don't have to have props to get students to see what you are talking about, but acting, on some level, as if what you are talking about is present, will help your students visualize its presence.
  - When I am describing something in a piece of literature, I sometimes *subtly* act it out.
    - You don't have to act out everything, but if you can put in pieces of action, you will catch the eye of students and break them from straight listening (which can lead to occasional daydreams).

- Add students in on the movement when you can, to break up the likely monotony of your simply talking.
  - When teaching comma rules, I often have students come forward to "act out" these rules using nothing more than their bodies and objects they have on their person such as books and pencils.

4. Illustrations

In kindergarten, I knew I wanted to be a teacher. Basing my early decision on a desire to write on the chalkboard whenever I pleased, I have now developed a more sophisticated educational drive. Besides, chalkboards have been replaced with white boards, dashing my early dreams to bits. Now instead of chalk handprints on the sides of our pants, we teachers can have blue, black, or red marker smudges on our hands.

Yet, the white board—available in most classroom spaces I have visited—is often under used.

I remember a teacher who would write one word on the board each class. That word wasn't necessarily more important than the rest he shared in the lecture; he just seemed to remember there was a board and a dry erase marker present in the classroom and think to use it at that moment.

Writing a key word here and there can be a helpful addition to your lecture. It can break from the vocal and give recognition, visually, to a term or idea's importance. But what I like to do most with my white board is use it to draw an illustration. An unforgettable illustration. *Why unforgettable*, you ask? (And you know it is important if I used a fragment on purpose.) *Unforgettable*, I answer, *because my drawing skills didn't progress past pre-school.*

Yes, my stick figures are sometimes unrecognizable. But drawing out something we are talking about in class makes the concept more memorable—even though (or especially because) the artwork is so horrid.

One of the best examples I can give is of Cletus, the two trick pony. For some reason, when I see a semicolon, I think of a horse's tail. Drawing a horse's behind on the white board, with a semi-colon tail, is my way of helping student remember the two uses for a semicolon. The example was so popular one year that Cletus found his way onto Facebook.

5. Storytelling

One of the reasons Cletus goes over so well is because he brings in an element of humor. Humor, emotion, personal accounts: these storytelling qualities are an excellent way to avoid the three complaints on lectures I mentioned at the start of my section.

I get lost in my thoughts and cannot pay attention.
Her voice tends to drone on, and I lose concentration.
I don't feel involved.

Again and again, I hear students say they like to know their teachers on some sort of personal level. You don't have to share your intimate life secrets: they don't even have to know what kind of breakfast cereal you prefer—but sharing some element of your life can show your passion and connection to the topic.

Storytelling is an art form in and of itself. A class in college on this art form would be quite beneficial for many careers, especially educators. Humor shows you are human; it connects the topic to something most people enjoy: laughter. Raw emotion (passion, sadness, some level of disgust) shows students the life of whatever you are talking about. I can remember reading "The Ones who Walk From Omelas" by Ursula K. Le Guin out loud to one of my literature classes. At one point in the story, the intense description of a mistreated child brought tears racing to my eyes. This unasked for emotion embarrassed me at first. "I'm sorry," I told them, my voice breaking as I tried to read on. "Don't be," one student said. They were all quiet, uncomfortable, pained. They should have been. I couldn't have brought this connection to the literature in any way other than my raw feelings being exposed.

We are not robots. Our subjects are not dead. So why do we present ourselves and our subjects such? Let your lectures live—while technology is grand, and while I use it often as a teaching aid, we teachers—our minds and our hearts—are still the stronghold of education. If we will allow our love of learning to come through; if we will remember our students are living, breathing, thinking beings who may or may not like what we are teaching (but should!), we can revitalize the lecture.

Part Two

Mark Hilliard

Is the Lecture a Viable Teaching Method?

At one time, the lecture held a place of honor and esteem in academia. Yet today, the lecture has been delegated to the basement, so to speak, in the inventory of viable teaching methodologies—stuffed away in old boxes with our platform shoes and leisure suits. But is that where it belongs, and why has it been so consigned?

The Oxford English Dictionary defines "lecture" as "an educational talk to an audience, especially one of students in a university," but it also offers the definition of "a lengthy reprimand or warning." Could it be that somewhere along the line of fine lecturing we somehow digressed from the first definition to definition two, and our "talks" to our students became the psychological equivalent of lengthy reprimands, more so than meaningful dialogue—"educational talks?"

I would hope that we could all say that we have experienced lectures that captured our attention: lecturers who captivated us with their words and experiential expressions. But, I know that we have all, likewise, experienced lectures that had the same negative effect as a reprimand on our intellectual capacity to learn to the extent that we shut out the speaker and transfigured our mind into a state of meaningless contemplation—day dreaming. As a result of a multiplicity of bad lectures over a period of time, I am afraid we have, in the words of my mother, "thrown out the baby with the bath water." We have all but eliminated the lecture from our repertoire of teaching and learning styles, and I am concerned that we are raising a generation of students and new teachers who might never experience, or learn how to offer, a quality lecture. This distresses me immensely and is the major reason for this exploration into whether or not the lecture is a viable teaching method.

Let's begin with an analysis of some of the broad, major components of a lecture, actually not of the lecture itself so much as all the elements that surround the lecture:

- the subject matter;
- the interest of the audience in the subject matter;
- the pre-knowledge and experiences of the audience and ability of the audience to comprehend, translate, and apply the information delivered in the lecture (which can relate to age, previous level of training or education, sex, cultural background, preconceived notions about the speaker or the subject matter, and a multitude of other characteristics which affect the ability of the audience to appropriately listen and learn);
- the time of day for the lecture;
- the environment or location of the lecture;
- the speaker;
- the knowledge of the speaker;
- the experiences of the speaker;
- the training of the speaker—on teaching and learning, and on the subject matter; and
- the ability of the speaker to relate to the audience and the audience to relate to the speaker.

1. The Subject Matter

While the subject matter is quite relevant in giving a lecture, I know from experience that a good lecturer can make any subject matter a valued and worthwhile encounter. As speakers, sometimes our topics are assigned—hopefully based on our area of expertise; sometimes we are able to select our topics from a pre-determined list; and sometimes the subject matter is ours for the choosing. At whatever the level of choice the lecturer has, it is important to either select a subject for which you have both knowledge and experience, or to create the time and opportunity to obtain some degree of advanced knowledge and experience before offering the lecture.

I cannot overemphasize the importance of some level of experiential expertise in offering a quality lecture. And while direct experience with the subject matter is incredibility beneficial, experience does not always have to be directly related to the topic, but quite often is simply a by-product of a multiplicity of life experiences that give you the ability to communicate effectively and meaningfully.

What we don't always understand is that each of our experiences becomes a part of our collective memory and is accessible to our brain to help us express a point, expand on a thought, provide a metaphor, or tell a story (even if these experiences do not directly relate to the subject matter), and these experiential expressions are needed to make our subject matter come alive. In practical terms, the more smells we smell, the more tastes we taste, the more sounds we hear, the more sights we see, and the more shapes and textures we touch, the more our experiences are expanded. And the more experiences, the better our ability to lecture.

By experiencing the smell of a pipe, the speaker is better able to describe smells. By traveling to a foreign county, the speaker is better able to speak on the excitement of travel. By experiencing a variety of emotions, the speaker is better able to express feelings. And by reading an assortment of books, the speaker is better able to express a variety of evocative words. Through our study, research, and active participation in life, we are better able to assemble our words into meaningful dialogue that will connect with the experiences of our audience.

2. The Interest of the Audience in the Subject Matter

I love the opportunity to speak before an audience whom I know feels an affection for me, and/or for the subject matter I will be discussing. But, if this is not the case, it is the lecturer's responsibility to create such interest with his words, his delivery of words, his actions, and his experiential sharing of the subject. A good lecturer should be able to enchant most any audience by drawing them into his world. How does he accomplish this task?

I like to use an excellent book as an example of how to draw the audience into a good lecture. I am a very critical critic of books. I have as many unfinished books on my shelves as finished ones. I have to be captivated within the first few pages of a book, or I simply will not go forward with reading it. And what do I look for in a book that corresponds to a good lecture? I wish to first be introduced to the big picture of the subject matter. Entice me, excite me, intrigue me with what you are going to share (the words used, the excitement or appropriate delivery of your words, the intellectual quality of your words, the gestures, etc.). Let me see that you are passionate about the subject and that you wish to bring me *into* the story you are about to share. Then give me some background—how you came about your knowledge (your experience), the benefits of listening to what you have to share (what makes the material both relevant and of interest to me—the audience, listener, or reader). Then go forward with the story—your lecture.

The lecturer must connect with his audience very quickly, and I suggest you do this by touching, at a minimum, three senses. I do not want to simply hear your words. I want to see them in *you*, hear them in *you*, and feel them in *you*. I want to smell and taste them. I want to experience the subject as you have experienced it—you become the experiential expression of the subject matter. And while it is always good to over prepare, do not over saturate your audience. Like a good stand-up comedian, go out on a good note with the audience wanting more. Sometimes that means stopping earlier than you had planned, maybe even leaving off a portion of your planned speech, because you see that you have your audience wishing for you to come back for another session.

3. The Pre-Knowledge and Experiences of the Audience, and Ability of the Audience to Comprehend, Translate, and Apply the Information Delivered in the Lecture *(which can relate to*

*age, previous level of training and education, sex, cultural back-
ground, preconceived notions about the speaker or the subject
matter, and a multiplicity of other characteristics which affect
the ability of the audience to appropriately listen and learn)*

Remember the stage of The Hilliard Circle of Teaching and
Learning in chapter three called Translation? Translation occurs
when the hearer is able to place the information delivered into
his personal way of thinking and acting. It is about introducing
the hearer to the subject matter at his level of pre-knowledge and
experiences and then creating an interest in the hearer so that he
wishes to add to that knowledge and so that he becomes excited
about expanding his experiences after hearing what the lecturer
has to say.

If the audience is likely to come without pre-knowledge because
of age, sex, or other demographically-based lack of awareness, the
lecturer is responsible to provide enough pre-knowledge to induce
an interest in the subject matter—sometimes we need to prep our
audience on the subject at hand before we begin to delve deeply.

How do we do this? First, find out all you can about your audience from individuals directly related to the program, through
research about the type of group you will address, or through personal interaction with the audience or class. If the lecture is to be
presented to a college class, the lecturer may simply email perti-
nent preliminary information to each student, and a portion of the
first class may be used to have students share about themselves.
If the lecture is more of a formal affair before a new audience, the
speaker may spend a few minutes providing some background information about the subject matter. Consider what questions you
might have originally asked when you began to study the subject,
and use those questions and answers in your introduction.

4. The Time of Day for the Lecture

As a professor for many years, I have my preference for when I
like to teach, and part of that preference is based on my personal

desires, while also, in part, based on when I believe I receive the most attention from my students. I am a 9:00 to 11:00 a.m. teacher. My second preference is between 3:00 and 6:00 p.m.

I most like to teach in the morning so I can get up, prepare, and go directly into the classroom with a focus on what I am to share—before other activities have pulled my attention away from my upcoming class and subject matter. I do not like to teach directly after lunch or late in the evening. My students tend to be a little too mellow (tired) immediately after lunch, and a little too restless (wanting to go home) later in the evening. Because of the nature of a lecture, the above times have become my recommendation for the best use of this teaching format.

I do, however, believe that by utilizing many of the suggestions that I share within this chapter, a teacher can overcome any time-of-day issues and offer a high quality lecture regardless. In fact, I find that, outside the typical classroom situation, I am often called to lecture during a luncheon meeting, or in the evening, making it even more important to call upon multiple sensory motivational techniques in order to capture my audience's attention when the time of day may fight against me. The lecturer must stimulate the audience into a heightened awareness with the same type of skill an athlete may use to gain and maintain his audience's attention.

5. The Environment or Location for the Lecture

Just as there are environments conducive to pleasure, sport, reverence, or romance, I believe there are also environments that are conducive to learning. Everything from proper lighting, to color psychology (the paint choices for the walls), to external sound control, to neatness and order, to the overall structure of a space—all play a role in providing a quality teaching and learning environment, and each type of learning can benefit from an appropriate, and sometimes different, setting. Creative learning can benefit from a structured, yet relaxed atmosphere. Highly intellectual learning can benefit from more formality. And philosophical learning enjoys a natural setting. But, if you do not have the best environment for the subject matter, you can create the environment with sensory words, stories, experiential expressions, enthusiasm, passion, gestures, or through questions and other means of building audience participation—which can be both active and passive in nature.

Examples of how to create a personal environment: if the lecturer is to represent the quality environment in and of himself, he must draw attention to self in an appropriate manner. Simple hand gestures, such as holding a hand over the heart, offer an environment of security and authenticity. Changing voice intensity can pull an audience back when their minds stray. Adding rhythm to the voice through the reading of poetry, a song, a verse, or a quote can capture the initial attention of the audience. The attire and overall image of the speaker can offer a formal or casual feel to the environment as desired. Good visuals can draw attention away from negative aspects of a space. Complimenting people in the audience, the town, or the organization can create an environment of familiarity and comfort, as can making the audience laugh. And moving about the stage gracefully and confidently, or walking toward or out into the audience, can secure the speaker as the element on which to concentrate. The most difficult problem to consider might be poor sound control; you must be aware of how you can use your voice or technology to eliminate this trouble. A good speaker can overcome most any negative environment.

6. The Speaker

The most important element in the lectureship equation is the speaker. What I mean by this is that a well-prepared speaker has the ability to make or break the lecture.

But what does well-prepared mean? It means that the speaker, to the best of his ability, has addressed all the other components in this list of elements that surround a lecture. Appropriate attention has been paid toward his personal knowledge and experience and his ability to relate with, and connect to, his audience; he has addressed the location and set-up for the lecture as much as possible; he has given attention to the time of day or at least the effect of the time of day on the audience; and he has a degree of knowledge and understanding of the make-up of the audience and how to connect them with the subject matter based on their pre-knowledge and their demographic composition. Unfortunately, very few lecturers take the time to address more than one or two of these issues.

All learning begins with sensory stimulation. Therefore, a good lecture needs to offer a variety of sensory stimulation to an array of audience sense-receptors. The speaker should consider ways in which to present opportunities for the audience not only to hear what is said, but to share in the experience through sight, touch, smell, and/or taste. I recommend the stimulation of *at least* three of the senses for every lecture—and not always the same three. I also believe it is possible to offer stimulation for all the senses in every lecture—more about this follows.

7. Stimulation through Visuals

In addition to the sound of our words, sight is often the other sensory stimulation we most often provide through the use of audio-visuals such as PowerPoint or an ever-changing new venue of electronic, media-based supply of technologic gadgetry. As a precursor to this new technology, at one time, my father used a white bed sheet, draped behind the podium, onto which an outline of each lesson was pre-written in large magic-marker letters—often in multiple colors. For the era of the 1960s, I found this technique very creative and effective. So think outside the *electric-box* when considering visuals.

In addition to electronic formats for visuals, a speaker may use handouts and posters, but attention must also be directed toward the use of personal gestures, hand motions, and facial expressions. Audiences like to pick up on emotional expressiveness in speakers, making it very important that these motions are appropriate and meaningfully communicated. Likewise, attention must be paid to the speaker's dress, image, and overall presence. For some audiences, the speaker must be in a suit and tie to bestow the appropriate level of expected credibility. At other times, the speaker must dress like the audience before him, which might be leisure attire, sporting clothing, or formalwear.

A perfect example of the importance of image as it ties to verbal presentation is music. At one time music was all about the sound. Today, with the advent of music videos, music is as much about the look as the sound. It is the same with the lecture, and all lecturers would do well to use the same psychology as used in a music video in preparing for any given talk. I believe the presentation style offered by the speaker, just like the style offered by the musician, is as important as the words spoken. And I must add that there is not any "one look fits all" formula for how a lecturer should look. It is a very personal learning experience to determine the best way for each lecturer to present himself. I recommend initially trying various styles, but settling with one that represents you at your very best and, early on, gaining input from people in the audience as to the style, image, and the presence you exude. Avoid anything that draws extreme attention to itself—a huge necklace, purple hair, a loud-colored article of clothing, an extreme style, etc.

8. Stimulation through Touch

The next most used sensory stimulation available to the lecturer is touch. This kinesthetic stimulation can be addressed via visuals that offer pseudo-textural appeal through a variety of computer-assisted graphic methodologies, or, in some instances, appropriate textural materials may be passed among the audience—a lesser effective method.

A better kinesthetic approach is what I call verbal-textural stimulation. Through a well-derived use of certain words, the speaker can describe a texture, a form, a shape, or a sensation in such a tactile way that the hearer can identify with the words and can, through cognitive sensory recall, actually "feel" what is expressed by the words.

This is why I will continue to express the importance of experience, on top of experience, on top of experience, as the key to providing quality lectures. Experience is what makes the lecture successful. If both the speaker and the audience have experienced a specific kinesthetic, textural, tactile encounter, choice words can re-stimulate this sense of touch. Become a collector and custodian of words: learn new words; find multiple words to express each sense through words. Then keep all these words in a word journal, and pull them out when creating a new lecture.

9. Stimulation through Smell and Taste

Almost never used in the thought process of preparing a lecture are concepts toward stimulating the senses of smell and taste via our words—unless the presentation is related to something like the culinary arts. So I will use the culinary arts as the formula for stimulating these two very important senses through our words. If I have tasted an absolutely lovely, seared on the outside, juicy on the inside, T-bone steak; one that comes to my table still *hissing* from just being removed from the hot, golden-red flame of the grill; where the smell entering my nostrils is of fresh, prime beef cooked medium, to perfection, with just the right touch of moist-pink tenderness, as I cut into it, I should be able to describe this experience so that individuals hearing me speak can taste and smell the steak with me. If, as the speaker, I have personally encountered this culinary process with artistic familiarity, I should be able to select the right words to express my experience to my audience. And if I am blessed, my audience will have likewise experienced this same occurrence, and just like with the verbal-textural stimulation, they will experience verbal-olfactory and/or verbal-gustatory stimulation, and my audience will actually smell and taste what I am speaking about via cognitive-sensory recall. If you don't believe this can occur, think of a recent dream in which you smelled an aroma or tasted a flavor, without the actual smell or flavor at your side. But, rather, the smell or flavor was provided to you via sensory expression through cognitive-sensory recall.

Think of the concept of an artist painting the picture of a lemon pie. If a viewer looks upon the painting and believes it to be appealing, it is art. If the viewer looks upon the painting and it makes him salivate, it is sensory design. Our words, through an appropriate training process, can become sensory design. Our words can cause the hearer to see, hear, feel, taste, and smell the subject matter. As a good lecturer, we, the speaker, become the sensory stimulation for our audience.

10. The Knowledge of the Speaker

While there is no substitute for knowledge, there are most certainly ingredients that, when added to knowledge, create a more dynamic lecture. I would place experience at the top of this list and will speak of it next. But here, let's speak of knowledge.

Knowledge comes in a variety of ways and through a variety of formats (self teaching, academic training, job experience, life learning, specialized research, etc.). There are speakers who are good generalists, some who are good specialists, and a few who are both. When taking on a new course to teach in my early career, in a topic I had never deeply studied or taught, I was told by my advisor, "Just always stay ahead of your students in your reading of the chapters, in your outside study of the topic, and in the activities and experiences to be discussed, and you become the expert." While I would prefer to be "way ahead" of the students in my knowledge and experiences of any class I am teaching, I thought this recommendation was valid advice and has served me well in always conducting new research before I teach a class. Now, in a way, I guess you could say I like to stay a step ahead of *myself*—I do not use the same notes from year to year, but always conduct new research to add to my current knowledge.

11. The Experiences of the Speaker

A good lecture is an expression of the intellectual, intuitive, and experiential capacities of the speaker. It requires the lecturer to place emotional significances into his words, his gestures, and even his personal image and style, supported by, and most beneficially pre-empted by, experience. There is a significant difference in "knowing something" and simply "knowing *about* something;" in knowing through "experiential learning" and in knowing through "simple book learning." There are no words that can express something accurately without the speaker, and hearer, having experienced what the words are trying to represent. Our words are defined by personal experience.

12. The Training of the Speaker—On Teaching and Learning, and on the Subject Matter

There are literally hundreds of variations of teaching and learning styles and philosophies, and I recommend all teachers and lecturers study some of these methodologies. But I also believe that all of these processes can be summed up, and simplified, into what I call "teaching and learning to the senses." If the lecturer can learn how to appropriately touch each of the senses of his audience, in each lecture, he will be successful. And the best way to learn how to do this is to methodically study and experience each of the senses as much as possible and journal about these experiences. Study the scientific and emotional concepts of taste and smell; then experience scores of tastes and smells. Learn words that describe various smells and tastes, stories that relate them to other things, colors that express them, and shapes that portray them. And do the same thing for the senses of touch, sight, and hearing. Learn various ways to describe sounds, words that illustrate touch, and words and expressions that articulate a variety of visuals.

13. The Ability of the Speaker to Relate to the Audience and the Audience to Relate to the Speaker

At some point, in each lecture experience, it is important for the speaker to relate to the audience. I typically like to walk among the crowd and meet people before I speak, sometimes without sharing that I am the speaker. The reading of the speaker's bio is also a way to help the audience relate to the speaker. The sharing of the bio is more than a ploy to impress the audience; it is a way to provide information to which they can relate: where did you go to school, where do you live, what organizations do you belong to (which they may also belong to), what have you written, what are some of your accomplishments and experiences, what connectivity do you have with their town and their lives, etc. A bio should be a poetic expression of your life experiences based on facts but also emotion. Re-do your bio every year, making changes and updates, and also re-do your bio to fit each particular audience—just as you would a resume directed to a specific business.

Another way to relate to the audience is through multiple styles of expression. Use humor, stories, poems, facts, readings, and letters, and avoid a monotone presentation. Look at your audience; move around, at least a bit.

Then comes relating the audience with the subject matter. By better knowing whom you are speaking to, it is much easier to share your talk in a manner that will capture their attention. If you are speaking to an audience who has purchased tickets to attend a birthday party for Hemingway, at the Hemingway Museum in Oak Park, they are there to listen to a talk about Hemingway, so your subject matter is already of interest. Talk about his poems, his stories, his wives, his adventures, his uniqueness, and make sure you share some details that may be new to the audience.

But what if the listeners are not Hemingway lovers? Then your first job is to remedy that fact quickly. Introduce them to the most exciting things about Hemingway first: share one of his best short stories; tell about his amazing adventures, of his life tragedies, and of his love of women and of exploration—and you will capture your audience.

Remember what I previously discussed about reading a good book—how would you begin a movie or book about Hemingway? What would the first chapter or the first three minutes of a movie offer? Consider these questions, and deliver that material in your introduction. You have about that same amount of time to capture your audience, if they are not familiar with your subject matter.

The Oxford Experience

As a part of my 2013 Summer Research Fellowship at Harris Manchester College, University of Oxford, I was privileged to interview two highly recommended lecturers. I asked them to share some of the methodologies they used to prepare, and share, a quality lecture. Notes from these interviews are below:

Dr. Stephen Gough

Professor of Diabetes and Consultant Physician, Oxford Centre for Diabetes, Endocrinology, and Metabolism (OCDEM), Churchill Hospital, Oxford; and Senior Research Fellow at Harris Manchester College, University of Oxford

- There is a purposeful formality about a lecture. It is not meant as an opportunity to simply "throw out" information that is already written, but it is meant to offer a balanced opinion about a topic.
- Rehearse the entire lecture before it happens, leaving nothing to chance. Try to make this take place in the actual space the lecture will occur.
- Know who your audience is, and prepare the lecture for that specific audience.
- Prepare and use a headline sentence that is simple and created to grab your audience. Think of how you would do this for a young person, of perhaps nine years of age. That is the type of sentence you are working toward to begin your talk—clean, simple, and meaningful, with a level of excitement.
- Incorporate effective pauses, and definitely give a pause before someone has to answer a question.
- Practice effectively and comfortably moving across the stage before the lecture occurs.
- If you are using slides or other visuals on one or more screens, talk to your slides: "As you can see on the left hand slide." Don't use a pointer.
- Minimize text on any visuals, and for slides use text colors such as clear dark blue on white. Don't overdo color on visuals.

- In addition to any audio visual needs, ask for a table, a glass of water, and, if desired, a lectern or podium.
- Various media outlets offer good examples of how to present a topic. Examine how they work to get a message across, and borrow from those methods.
- Spend as much time, or more, on how to convey your message, as on the actual message.
- Always examine your lecture after it is complete for weak points, strengths, changes you need to make, etc.

Dr. Amanda Palmer

Head of the Institute of Human Sciences at Oxford; Director of Studies (Human Sciences) at Harris Manchester College, University of Oxford; Lecturer in Sociology at St Catherine's College, University of Oxford

- Involve the audience with the lecture through questions:
    - Why do you think that is so?
    - Let's pull the details of this situation out together.
    - Help me list the information on the board.
    - What do you make of the theory?
- Use visual prompts, which may be electronic or non-electronic visuals prepared and shared to stimulate the audience. These prompts may be as simple as bullet points to move the audience from one piece of information to the next.
- Find a thread that connects the various aspects of your lesson. This helps keep the audience engaged with the entire talk.
- Move around, wander about the space, not to the point of distraction, but the activity of movement helps engage and keep the audience engaged.
- Interview someone related to a topic (a musician, etc.). Present the interview questions and answers to the audience in text form. Then through questions and answers, engage the audience in a conversation about the interview.
- Physically place yourself on the same level as your audience—not on a raised platform.

- Invite questions, even in a lecture, and walk around making eye contact with the audience to encourage questions.
- Avoid harsh lighting when possible—use soft lighting.

Final Thoughts—Art of the Lecture

Put into practice, the directives from this chapter will forever change the interest level of your lecture, and therefore its value. As an educator, you have important knowledge to share; but if no one listens, the worth of that knowledge moves no further than your own mind. The lecture is still a valid method of information transference, but only if we take the time to rethink our objectives, techniques, and desired outcomes.

Mark and Jessa on the grounds of Harris Manchester College

Chapter 7
Personal Application
Using The Hilliard Circle of Teaching and Learning in the Classroom

A Need for Practical Examples

Jessa Sexton

When reading educational philosophies, my initial ideas often hinge around the thoughts, *Well, that's nice, but how can I do it in my classroom?* Too many times I have read books and articles with brilliant ideas, but no practical information on how I can apply those ideas to my teaching. Sometimes this deficiency leaves me mulling over great ideas only to leave them as that—ideas.

We want The Hilliard Circle of Teaching and Learning to be more than great ideas; we want this philosophy to have a place in your personal curriculum. This next section will suggest ways to incorporate the senses into your teaching, give you a sample learning plan for a unit on health following The Circle, provide a learning plan chart for your use, and supply directives for writing teaching and learning goals that use The Circle.

Reflecting on the Senses

Jessa Sexton

The first levels of The Hilliard Circle involve connecting the topic with the students' senses. In our study, teachers of all disciplines have found this daunting: math, literature, art, science, design, history, technology—even after reading the charts we provided on how to incorporate each sense into lessons, educators in each field of study may still feel overwhelmed by the task of stimulating student senses.

I think the first step is for us, as educators, to reflect on the sensory expressions associated with our disciplines. Hopefully the charts below can get you started as you brainstorm your own lists of the senses involved in your field.

Take the time to consider what elements connect to each of the senses of your discipline. Then, take your reflection one step further to ponder the spiritual or emotional elements; remember that students prefer a teacher who is passionate about a topic. What drew you to your field in the first place, and what feelings and emotions drive you further in your continued learning and teaching?

How to Engage Student Senses

Jessa Sexton

Once you have identified how the senses connect with your learning, you are better prepared to present sensory stimulations for your students. For seven years, I was fortunate enough to teach college classes that met only once a week. Challenging myself to open each class with an activity or a moment of reflection that would touch an often overlooked sense of my students was not as difficult as if I were seeing the same students each day. Instead of intimidating yourself by such a prospect, perhaps your first goal should be to begin each new unit at the start of The Hilliard Circle.

When I teach John Steinbeck's *The Pearl*, I have the students fill out a chart showing how different instances in the first chapter touch each of their senses, including the spiritual sense. The theme of injustice present throughout the book is made tangible and sensual as the students reflect on the poor man's breakfast of tasteless rice cakes versus the rich doctor's bacon and chocolate. Having these foods available will further activate their connection with an ongoing theme in the novel.

Romeo and Juliet has a line that is better understood by a sensory experiment. "A rose by any other word would smell as sweet," Juliet says as she commiserates having fallen in love with a boy who bears the name of her enemy. I brought in a bottle of rose lotion—the kind that smelled exactly like a crushed rose petal—and put it on. I had a student smell and relate to the class what the lotion smelled like before I walked around and let them all agree: the lotion smelled like its name, rose. Then I asked my student to consider my renaming it to "burnt tire." How did it smell now? After her awkward look and timid sniff, she admitted, "It still smells like a rose." And what if I called it "wet dog," how did it smell with that name? The student stood by her first word; it smelled like a rose. The students smelled Shakespeare's meaning: a name does not define makeup. (A year after this lesson, I asked a student what she remembered about the play; she verbally repeated the experiment with the lotion and explained the meaning of this classic line. Four years later, a student emailed me saying she was able to finish the quote on a college orientation tour when no one else could. She thought of the lotion and of me; her memory of this event kept strong all that time.)

Though I loved algebra, I remember struggling with geometry because I am not very spatial. Staring at a square on a paper and trying to imagine it as an actual three-dimensional object with not only a circumference but also an *area* would have been so much easier if I could have touched a better representation of the shape.

Many students, especially the light of stomach, dread the day of dissection. I can still smell the formaldehyde when I walk into my

151

old high school science classes and remember holding my breath as biology became real—and really gross—to me. Science fair experiments were the only part of this course I truly looked forward to; the hands-on approach helped me understand concepts I had previously only read about. When students learn about the Punnett square, let them smell, touch, and see plants representing the recessive and dominant genes instead of simply looking at the drawings in their textbooks.

History is alive! Or at least we tell people that, but how often do we make it so? Many history teachers make the effort to show film clips about their lessons, yet stop there. What were the sights, sounds, smells, tastes, and items to touch of the period you are talking about? Give your students a chance to be transported, as physically as possible without a time machine, to the past.

These are just some examples of how several different disciplines can engage students by connecting with their senses. Next I want to share experiences from two other educators, both in the English as a second language field.

Hannah Cregg

When teaching imperatives, I use recipes: usually a no-bake cookie recipe. I bring in the cookies, and, of course, the students want to eat them right then and there. But instead, we go through the steps of the recipe; at the end, they get to eat the cookies that they have made. As we are baking I'll give brief explanations on the commands and instructions, with more in depth information on the imperative form at the end.

When I'm teaching shapes to preschoolers, I use giant foam shapes and put them on the floor. I then play songs in English (trying to include some songs that sing about shapes too). When the music stops, the children find a shape and stand on it. Then I say something like, "I see a star" (if they are on the star), and then they repeat. We play this a few times so that they are learning while being active.

My goal when teaching ESL is not that the students simply translate from one language to another but that they are able to learn and truly know English: using all learning styles, I try to get them to think in this language from an early age with videos, songs (which work really well for most students), games, flashcards, worksheets, presentations, and projects that involve the students constructing things and following directions throughout the process.

Alex Beene

For those teaching a new language to a classroom of learners, the term "language immersion" is commonly used. For classes with a medium level of difficulty, this is a powerful concept, as it forces learners into an environment where conversation is primarily carried out in the newly-acquired language.

When a student is learning English as a second language, a different term should be used, which I find very helpful in terms of planning and instruction: "cultural immersion." ESL is not just about being able to grasp the correction pronunciation of words and proper conjugation of verb actions, but also about the Western culture that surrounds the meaning of sentences used in daily life.

How can cultural immersion be effectively presented? The easiest way for students to get a better understanding of new words and ideas is by linking those to other senses. Let's say your classroom is doing a section on eating out in a typical American restaurant. Some instructors would simply go over the terminology in the book, having students repeat the learned information and moving on to the next section. The likelihood of the student actually remembering the material entirely—or even just parts of it—is very low.

Now, instead of doing a simple book-and-pencil setting, picture a classroom that's been turned into a mock restaurant. Design the desks in circles to feel like a table, and print out small menus.

You can have a small selection of food items from which to order and even provide some fake money for them to pay with after the meal's conclusion.

Through this cultural immersion, you've done a few things. You involved their smell and taste in the learning, which is great. The

Visual and Fine Arts	Performing Arts
Smell media used in art; visual art can evoke the aromatic ambiance of various environments; printing inks; paper; Sharpie pens; rubber cement; spray mount	**Smells** various instrument smells (wood, metal, plastic; old, new); makeup; sweat; the heat given off from a spotlight; the mustiness of stored costumes and uniforms; the odor of a full versus empty concert hall or theatre; grass on the marching field; items used as props and backdrops; the curtain
Taste period or culturally-appropriate cuisine and foods represented in still life; proper use of color and image—a bright, juicy orange should produce a "taste" sensation or at least a response from the salivary glands; holding a paintbrush in your mouth; experiencing the foods of a restaurant before you work on their ad campaign	**Tastes** reed and/or mouthpiece; prop food (real or pantomimed—should seem real); teas to soothe and prepare the throat; water; meals with fellow performers on tour or between practices
Sight painting; printmaking; drawing; sculpture; computers; printers; paintbrushes; various media used in art; color; fonts; hues; shapes; typography...everything about the discipline relates to visual	**Visuals** images or shapes created by band members on a field show; costumes, wigs, makeup, uniforms; props; backdrops; lighting; natural and/or artificial light; visual cues from a director; the distinct directing pattern of your conductor; sheets of music; scripts; lines
Sounds charcoal on paper; brush on canvas; pen nib scratch; printing presses running; clicking of mouse and keyboards; whirring of computer and scanner; music—most designers listen to music that suits the mood of the project	**Sounds** music; song; voices; accents; commands from a director; the unfortunate squeak of an instrument or voice; vocal exercises; the sound of your voice as you learn your lines; crescendos and diminuendos; microphones or voice projections without such technology
Touch the feel, as well as the look, of an engraved or etched plate vs. a woodcut block vs. a silk screen; movement and muscle memory are important skills to acquire in art—drawing with a movement from the shoulder rather than the wrist or fingers; feel of papers and inks; keyboard and mouse; pain of slicing your finger while trimming and mounting a project	**Touch** movement needed to create music with breath, sticks, voice, etc.; marching; dancing; makeup; texture of costumes, wigs, uniforms; feeling of props; your chair during a concert or the field under your feet in marching band; sheets of music; the heat given off from a spotlight; scripts; movement on the stage; stage directions; physical interaction with other actors in a scene; facial expressions

Portions of these sense charts were shared with us by the following educators:

English names of the food items available will stick with them better because different senses were triggered in the lesson. More importantly, you've made the setting fun and social. Sitting around a table, students could talk to one another, laugh, and discuss some English-speaking elements of the area that cause them problems or they find easy.

History

Smells

blood or gunpowder on a battlefield; a candle as the only indoor lighting; kerosene for old lamps or heat; moth balls (once used to protect clothing); the earth; plants that are now used for medicine; antiques; old books; food smells that are meant to age (cheese, quality-aged meats, wine, liquors, cigars); ink; historic medicines (caster oil, old liniments); old containers (whiskey barrel, medicine, snuff, pipe tobacco, flour, perfumes, nails); an old house; words that express historic smells

Tastes

popular food items from various times; foods traditionally cured by salt or fire-dried; ways old food or drinks were stored or served (big mouth glass milk jug) and how containers affect taste; metaphorical bad taste in clothing or hair styles; trends in foods through time (lard vs butter vs no-transfat spreads); tastes of home-made items vs. commercially or mass production items; old style perked coffee vs. new style brewing; brewed tea vs. instant tea or other such items; words that express historic tastes

Visuals

Tombstones and graveyards (for various classes of people and cultures); historic markers and sights; art or book illustrations from various periods of time (the Book of Kells, Divinci, Monet); old photographs; maps; clothing or hats throughout time (or photos of such); old medicine bottles; old communication devices; old films and photos (space travel, battle scenes, old buildings then and now); items in museums; aging (visit to nursing home or a visiting senior speaker)

Sounds

words from an old journal; historic stories; old speeches or poems; good historic novels; music from various periods of time (instrumental and vocal); the quality of music from various devices (vinyl records, 8-tracks, real-to-reel, cassette tape, CD, iPod, etc.); nature sounds (not heard in many city environments today); historic visiting speakers

Touch

antiques; historic clothing, hats, bedding, fabric (old polyester, new micro-fiber, cotton, silk); historic tools or farm implements; kitchen implements; artifacts; historically used metals, woods, building materials; old books; writing implements (typewriters, pencils, quill pens); touching history through old journals, speeches, songs, poems; layers of paint or stain on old furniture

Bruce Bezaire, Paula Hanback, Dr. Jay Sexton, and Emily Waller.

Writing and Literature	Wellness
Smells Ink; pencil shavings; an eraser; the smell a laptop gives off as it heats from prolonged use; paper; the musty-sweet smell of an old book; experiencing the smells that are created by solid imagery in writing	**Smells** aroma therapy or candles to relax; the smell of plants and flowers that might be good or bad for you; various foods and their effect on the psyche; the smell of tobacco and how it may smell good or may irritate; the smell of sweat and what it means for the body; fresh, tilled earth and soil and their benefits to animal and human-kind; pheromones and their effect on human sexuality; the meaning of various atmospheric smells (rain, heat); natural vs. artificial smells; the smell and effect of allergy-causing agents
Tastes hot tea to mellow you as you ponder compli-cated reading; hot coffee to keep you awake as you burn the midnight oil to finish an essay; the desire to try the foods eaten by the characters in your book; the taste of your fingernails as you nervously turn in or receive a graded piece of your writing; learning to describe tastes with your words; becoming hungry because of well-worded imagery	**Tastes** foods that are good and bad for health; the various flavors of fruits, veggies, and herbs; the tastes of water (flavored, with minerals, no minerals, etc.); natural tastes vs. artificial tastes; alcohol, benefits and negative effects; the taste and purpose for salt and sugar; the difference in the tastes of protein, carbs, fat and how they are used by the body; the benefits and dangers of fasting
Visuals different levels of books stacked on a shelf; hardcovers versus paperbacks; the creased cor-ners of a book reminding you of a particularly well-worded passage; pens; paper; computers; printers; color; the larger first letter of every new chapter; the images you put in your head as the story unfolds; magazines; newsprint; different fonts; the color ink of your professor's corrections on your essay; a highlighted passage	**Visuals** examples or photos of food items from each food group; photos of muscle tone or physical examples to differentiate mass, tone, fat; color psychology and color theory; the emotional ef-fects of art; examples of various types, and ben-efits of, light; various atmospheric conditions and their meaning; using fire to burn various items to represent the burning of calories
Sounds the tap-tap-taping of the keyboard or the scratching of a writing utensil on paper; the dragging of a book being pulled off of a shelf; swooshing as you turn the pages of a book; slight crackling of the spine of a new book as it is opened for the first time; sighs and other sounds of frustration during the writer's revision stages; the effects of solid imagery letting you hear, in your head, the descriptions	**Sounds** the sound of various exercise equipment; nature sounds vs. equipment and other manmade sounds; the benefits and effects of music or poetry on heart rate; the various types of breathing, the sound and effect on the body; prayer or words of affirmation and their benefits psychological, physical, or spiritual; silence and meditation for relaxation; interpreting verbal tone
Touch knots and ridges on the fingers from holding a pen or pencil for a long time; beveled edges of an old book; raised fonts; the elevated markers on the f and j key of the keyboard guiding hands to their starting position; dragging your finger across the text to keep your place as you read; the mad crumpling of a poor draft followed by the toss at the wastebasket; the feel of a book you've been waiting to read; the weight of a book bag laden with texts; the heat of the laptop; that reach of the pinky to the delete button	**Touch** examples of various exercises (hiking, biking, aerobics, yoga, dance, resistance exercises); massage therapy; the wellness benefits of paint-ing, drawing, or other physical artistic activities; the benefits of hugging; how we transfer germs and disease through touch; how we transfer affection or aggression with touch; gardening or other manual activity which has multiple well-ness benefits to humankind and the earth

Math	Science
Smells your eraser wearing away as you try and retry a complex equation; dry erase markers or chalk the teacher uses to show examples; pencil lead; textbook odor; money (fresh bills vs used bills)	**Smells** formaldehyde; chemicals mixing; gas for the Bunsen burner; plant life; class pet; latex and powder smell on your hands when you remove gloves; wafting instead of inhaling
Tastes recipes and food preparation; measuring flavors; fraction and percentage learning with food (such the various colors in a bag of M&Ms); dehydrated foods (decreasing moisture and weight); wood, eraser, or plastic as you chew on your writing utensil	**Tastes** many foods and beverages created because of scientific discoveries; not being allowed to taste chemicals in lab; medicines; herbal remedies and their scientific validity; the fives tastes (bitter, sour, sweet, salty, savory)
Visuals chalk dust on the clothing or dry erase markers on the hands; Greek letters; shapes; rulers; compass; protractors; x; pencils; the mathematical standard symbols such as = + − x /; numbers; graph paper; lines; environmental math (numbers of offspring for various animals, symmetry in nature, numbers of leaves or limbs or blades of grass); distance; money; models	**Visuals** beakers; dissected animals; charts and graphs; safety goggles; flames; liquids changing colors in a flask; explosions; science fair boards; rocks; lab tables; emergency eye wash station; bright flash of burning magnesium; various demonstrations; graphs and charts; models
Sounds clicking of a calculator; moans of defeat; shouts of victory; whispers to a neighboring peer or your teacher for clarity; flipping of pages to the back of the textbook to check your answers; the rubbing of an eraser over a mistake; clink of coins or rustling of paper bills; counting (out loud or in the head, by 1s, 5s, 10s, 20s, etc); the language and terms of math	**Sounds** bubbling; whoosh of gas through the Bunsen burner; clanking of test tubes against each other; buzz of electricity; various sounds of electronics and other inventions
Touch hand supporting the head as you stare down a word problem; buttons of a calculator; heat coming off of your laptop; dusty chalk; wooden versus plastic rulers; holding a three-dimensional shape; sliding the rings on the abacus; pointy end of a compass, writing utensils, the process of writing and erasing; the movement of the student to the teacher's desk with questions or the teacher to the student with answers; making graphs and charts	**Touch** cold scalpel; tightness of safety goggles; tongs to grab test tubes; heat from Bunsen burner; lab coat material; dry hands from continual washing; hands-on activities; touching a patient

Using the Hilliard Circle of Teaching and Learning

Jessa Sexton

The following are four sections that may help you use The Circle in your own teaching and learning processes. The first is a listing of terminology you can use to set up your course or unit objectives. By considering what the learner will (TLW) accomplish by the end of a unit or course, you can begin to set up learning plans using The Circle to reach these goals: called the Mastery of Skills and Knowledge expected of our students. The second is a chart that is an example of a health unit learning plan following The Hilliard Circle. Third, a blank learning plan chart is provided for you to copy and use. Finally, we have shared a few sample rubrics.

Mastery of Skills and Knowledge Guide

Every teacher should create a list of skills and knowledge that a student should have and know in order to successfully complete each course taught. By using similar wording from several different categories noted here, the teacher can identify the level at which a student truly understands a specific topic. As with Bloom's Taxonomy, each level is higher in critical thinking and learning than the previous, so teachers should try to use some assessment wording from the lower and higher levels.

To shorten some of the descriptions, I have used TTW (The Teacher Will) and TLW (The Learner Will) to show the responsibilities or goals of each in this teaching and learning process.

Sampling of Wording

Stimulation

(The teacher enters the circle of learning by creating a stimulus, or by providing an opportunity for stimulation to occur, that produces a sense perception by the student.)

- TTW stimulate –
- TTW touch (emotionally or physically) –
- TTW read –
- TTW show –
- TTW say –
- TTW express –
- TTW question –
- TTW model –
- TTW explain –
- TTW describe –
- TTW do –

Sensation

(All learning begins with an initial contact with one or more of the senses. This does not, however, mean that any cognition has necessarily occurred at this point; teachers must learn to stimulate various senses.)

- TTW produce something that the student will touch.
- TTW produce something that the student will taste.
- TTW produce something that the student will smell.
- TTW produce something that the student will see.
- TTW produce something that the student will hear.
- TTW produce something that the student will feel.
- TTW produce something with which the student will become spiritually or metaphysically connected.

Reaction

(After a sensation occurs, there may or may not be a reaction based on the stimulation, but with appropriate training teachers can help positively direct student reactions.)

- TLW become interested.
- TLW become engaged.
- TLW become excited.
- TLW become inspired.
- TLW be aroused.

- TLW be touched.
- TLW be moved.
- TLW be motivated.

Identification

(At this level, learning occurs–it is, however, the lowest level of learning.)

- TLW define –
- TLW list –
- TLW recall –
- TLW record –
- TLW name –
- TLW match –
- TLW state –
- TLW write –
- TLW memorize –

Exploration Level

(The more meaningful levels of learning begin to occur as a student becomes actively involved in research and exploration.)

- TLW research –
- TLW investigate –
- TLW explore –
- TLW question –
- TLW find answers to –
- TLW process –
- TLW compare –
- TLW inspect –

Translation Level

(For deep meaning to occur, students must be able to make information personally relevant and understandable.)

- TLW convert –
- TLW apply –
- TLW transfer –

- TLW conclude –
- TLW reorder –
- TLW render –
- TLW change –
- TLW practically apply –
- TLW distinguish between –
- TLW describe in his or her own words –
- TLW explain in his or her own words –
- TLW summarize in his or her own words –
- TLW contrast –
- TLW compare –
- TLW categorize –
- TLW classify –
- TLW examine –
- TLW take _____ apart and _____

Utilization Level

(Students must have the opportunity to make something new and beneficial out of what they have learned.)

- TLW utilize –
- TLW advise –
- TLW prescribe –
- TLW invent –
- TLW test –
- TLW answer –
- TLW model –
- TLW accomplish _____ task
- TLW apply –
- TLW illustrate –
- TLW demonstrate –
- TLW solve –
- TLW use –
- TLW create –
- TLW design –
- TLW re-design –
- TLW plan –

- TLW revise –
- TLW produce –
- TLW assemble –
- TLW hypothesize –
- TLW formulate –

Justification Level

(For higher learning to occur, students must be able to prove their case based on solid research and factual information.)

- TLW prove –
- TLW appraise –
- TLW confirm value of or in –
- TLW judge –
- TLW rationalize –
- TLW measure –
- TLW recommend –
- TLW justify –
- TLW substantiate –
- TLW evaluate –
- TLW validate –
- TLW defend –

Adaptation Level

(If justification cannot be given, students must be able to make appropriate changes as needed.)

- TLW accommodate –
- TLW re-model –
- TLW re-design –
- TLW re-align –
- TLW re-work –
- TLW renovate –
- TLW retrofit –
- TLW amend –
- TLW revise –
- TLW adjust –

- TLW change –
- TLW modify –
- TLW vary –

Presentation Level

(Only through appropriate opportunities to express and present what has been learned, can students truly obtain the ability to effectively communicate what they know to others.)

- TLW effectively communicate –
- TLW appropriately convey –
- TLW explain in detail –
- TLW aptly impart wisdom –
- TLW express with meaning and detail –
- TLW expound with confidence –
- TLW perform with proficiency –
- TLW correctly portray –
- TLW effectively illustrate –
- TLW demonstrate with skill and knowledge –

Instruction Level

(The highest level of learning occurs when the student becomes the teacher—when the student has such a mastery of skills and knowledge that he or she is able to teach others how to do what he or she can do.)

- TLW become an expert in _____ and be able to expertly teach others to –
- TLW expressively teach or show others how to –
- TLW effectively instruct others to –
- TLW share his or her mastery of –
- TLW efficiently oversee the instruction of –
- TLW effectively manage others, having the skills and knowledge of those he or she manages and the ability to communicate both.

Mastery of Skills and Knowledge Examples

Jessa Sexton

Fundamentals of Speech

- Identification: TLW (The Learner Will) be able to list and define important vocabulary connected to communication (ex: four elements of communication, major speech parts).
- Exploration: TLW will research and explore communication barriers, lessons learned in unexpected areas, famous speakers and speeches, and several elements of communication.
- Translation: TLW apply his/her research and deeper understanding of this research to create speeches and fact sheets. (It is a goal of this course that the fact sheets will move from summary to translation.)
- Utilization: TLW be able to create outlines for speeches by categorizing and assembling information, both from his/her experiences and his/her research.
- Utilization: TLW use his/her creativity and communication skills to work through several class activities including impromptu presentations.
- Identification/Justification/Adaptation: TLW identify elements of famous speeches that make it "poor" or "good," justify his/her reasons for this judgment, and modify (or suggest modifications for) those elements to improve the speech. The student will also have to make adjustments to his/her own speech outlines in consideration of the particular intended audience before presenting.
- Presentation: TLW express his/her research and opinions on several topics through presentation.
- Instruction: TLW pick a particular relationship and research its communication difficulties. Through this experience, the student will become the class expert on the communication barriers of this relationship and will share this information with the class.

- Instruction: TLW pick a particular famous speaker and research his/her life and speeches and then teach the class what can be learned and applied to life and communication skills from this research.

Through the mastery of these skills, students will be able to reflect more deeply on communication skills in the classroom and in the world, produce speeches that are clearer and more concise, and tackle personal and professional presentations with more confidence.

Composition I

- Identification: TLW (The Learner Will) be able to name various rules in writing.
- Exploration: TLW will research and explore different elements of writing and literature through various readings.
- Exploration: TLW question the elements in literature.
- Utilization/Translation: TLW apply his/her research through writing a research paper of his/her conclusions.
- Utilization/Translation: TLW be able to create outlines for possible paper assignments by categorizing and assembling information.
- Utilization: TLW assemble facts and opinions to create a valid argument.
- Utilization: TLW use his/her creativity and grammar skills through writings, both formal and creative, and through presentations.
- Identification/Justification/Adaptation: TLW identify elements of writing that make it "poor," justify his/her reasons for this judgment, and modify (or suggest modifications for) those elements to improve the paper. This process will take place with example writings as well as the student's own writing.
- Presentation: TLW share research with the class.
- Instruction: TLW show the class methods to teach various grammar and/or writing skills.

Through the mastery of these skills, students will be able to reflect more deeply on literature, produce writing that is grammatically correct, tackle personal and professional writing projects with more confidence, and expand their thinking by making less obvious connections with literature and the current world.

HCTL Level	Learning Plan for Healthy Lifestyle Choices
Stimulation	*Teacher stimulates student by bringing in a basket of colorful fruits and vegetables.* *Key Words: inspire, engage, big picture, motivate, interest*
Sensation	*Which sense will the stimulation contact? The teacher lets the students look at, touch, and eat some of the foods in the basket—connecting to the sense of sight, touch, taste, and smell.* *Key Words: taste, touch, smell, sight, sound, emotional/ spiritual*
Reaction	*The students may respond with certain facial expressions based on how sweet or sour the foods are or with words such as "yum" and "blech."* *Key Words: negative, positive, neutral (the least desired response)*
Identification	*Students initially categorize the fruits and veggies by name, shape, color, size, texture, and taste qualities. (Notice the brightness and colorful nature of these healthy foods!) Facts on calories, food groups, and basic dietary information is shared.* *Key Words: label, define, list, name, date, record*
Exploration	*The student researches whether or not food colors, textures, etc. relate to nutrition and quality. The student investigates by going to a fast food restaurant known for unhealthy foods and searches for the healthiest foods he can find on the menu. Some research is needed. Just how "healthy" is the item each student picked? What is the most unhealthy item offered? After the exploration, students discuss in groups how easy it is to eat and live in an unhealthy manner.* *Key Words: research, observe, search, investigate, question, compare, study, discuss*

HCTL Level	Learning Plan for Healthy Lifestyle Choices
Translation	*The student personalizes the material by making connections to his own life. Applying what he knows about healthy and unhealthy foods, he interprets elements of his lifestyle (both eating habits and activities) that are healthy or unhealthy by categorizing them accordingly.* *Key words: apply, interpret, paraphrase, deduce, conclude*
Utilization	*Student uses skills and knowledge learned so far to create a healthy living plan he must follow for a set period of time.* *Key words: design, invent, make a portfolio, produce an answer to a problem, create*
Justification	*Using information from the exploration research, the student defends his plan on its healthy merits. (Drinking fewer soft drinks lowers calorie intake, which is a documented way to lose weight.)* *Key words: defend, support, critique, review, assess*
Adaptation	*After the set time period is over, the student makes changes based on how realistic or unrealistic the plan would be to implement for long periods of time.* *Key words: alter, modify, rewrite, revise, remodel, edit*
Presentation	*Student formally presents findings to share with others what he has learned about being healthy.* *Key words: communicate, share, demonstrate, explain, express, enlighten*
Instruction	*Students instruct each other on activities (yoga, meditation, aerobics, how to make a fruit salad) that can improve their health.* *Key words: guide, mentor, instruct, oversee, tutor*

HCTL Level	_____ Learning Plan
Stimulation	*Key Words: inspire, engage, big picture, motivate, interest*
Sensation	*Key Words: taste, touch, smell, sight, sound, emotional/ spiritual*
Reaction	*Key Words: negative, positive, neutral (the least desired response)*
Identification	*Key Words: label, define, list, name, date, record*
Exploration	*Key Words: research, observe, search, investigate, question, compare, study, discuss*

Feel free to photocopy this chart for your planning purposes.

HCTL Level	_____ Learning Plan
Translation	 *Key words: apply, interpret, paraphrase, deduce, conclude*
Utilization	 *Key words: design, invent, make a portfolio, produce an answer to a problem, create*
Justification	 *Key words: defend, support, critique, review, assess*
Adaptation	 *Key words: alter, modify, rewrite, revise, remodel, edit*
Presentation	 *Key words: communicate, share, demonstrate, explain, express, enlighten*
Instruction	 *Key words: guide, mentor, instruct, oversee, tutor*

Passage Reading

Pick and present a great speech or a passage of writing perfect for oral presentation.

I will grade you with this rubric:

Sight - Eye contact: *Student makes eye contact with various people in the audience, does not simply stare at his/her sheet or something inanimate.*	
Touch - Handout: *Student gives a copy of his/her passage or speech to the teacher with correct MLA reference.*	
Sound – Voice: *Teacher can hear the student (volume) and understand what he/she says (clarity / diction / speed).*	
Taste – Introduction: *Student gives a 1-4 sentence introduction telling the author of the passage and explaining the reason it is worthy (good taste) – why the student picked it.*	
Smell – Preparedness: *Student comes to class with an aroma of preparedness: does not have to make copies when he/she gets to class, presents as if he/she has read over the passage before–these elements help the speech not "stink."*	
Total Points:	/25 points
Student's Name:	

Famous Speaker Informational Speech Rubric
Sight - Eye contact and PowerPoint: **Student makes eye contact with various people in the audience, does not simply stare at his/her sheet.* **PowerPoint is not too cluttered, has appropriate use of art, and guides audience through the speech with correct MLA.*
Touch - Handout: Student gives this rubric, a copy of the PowerPoint, and a copy of the speech if the PowerPoint is not all the student is using for presentation. Appropriate MLA is used.
Sound – Voice: Teacher can hear the student (volume) and understand what he/she says (clarity / diction / speed).
Smell – Preparedness: Student comes to class with an aroma of preparedness: does not have to make copies when he/she gets to class, presents as if he/she has read over the speech before–these elements help the speech not "stink." Also, the speech is emailed to the professor by 3pm the day before the due date. (Emailed later or updated drafts emailed later = reduction of points.)
Taste: Content (30 points) Content follows flow of one of the attached outlines, giving due attention to the following information: basic information on the speaker's life, portions of the speaker's work with topics chosen and possible whys; portions of the speaker's work with comments on style of writing or delivery (with a video or audio example), and things a speaker today can learn from this speaker: all of this must be backed up with references.
Senses: Student must touch 2 senses of his/her audience BEYOND the PowerPoint as sight.
References (20 points): Student gives MLA references to his/her sources in the speech and on a references slide. Student must use at least 7 sources, at least 1 should be a video or sound bite source, and at least 2 must be a hard source (such as a magazine, book, etc).
Introduction / Conclusion / Transitions: Introduction grabs audience's attention and has a thesis that outlines the main topics of the speech. The conclusion sums up and leaves the audience thinking, feeling, or reflecting with a resonating final moment. Transitions are used to guide the audience through the main points, creating flow.
Total Points: */110*

Theme Paper Rubric	
	Advanced 9-10
Mechanics and Grammar	*0-3 mistakes*
Appearance	• *Typed* • *Correct heading (name, teacher name, class name, date)* • *title* • *double spaced* • *paragraphs indented* • *All subsequent pages carry student's last name and page number in upper right hand corner.* • *This rubric is stapled to the back of the paper.*
Content (Literature) *(20 points)*	*All elements of literature (2 poems, 2 short stories, one novel) are described and clearly connected to theme **with specific examples from the text**.*
MLA	• *All references are cited.* • *All quotes give exact page numbers (done in MLA style).* • *Block quotes (if used) are correct.* • *All references are cited correctly (perhaps with 1 mistake) in a separate works cited page.*
Intro/Conclusion *And Thesis Statement*	• *Introduction and conclusion are full paragraphs (4+sentences).* • *Intro gets the reader ready by introducing main elements of the theme.* • *Conclusion does not simply "sum up;" it really looks into the importance of the theme and shows depth of thought.* • *Thesis is last sentence in intro.* • *Thesis names the theme and the main points of the paper.* • *Thesis is an obvious outline of paper.*
Flow	• *Each section of the paper flows into the next.* • *Entire paper is one cohesive unit.* • *Transition sentences guide reader through.*
On Time / Page limit	• *Final Draft turned in during class.* • *Final Draft is **7-11** pages of writing. (Works Cited can start on page **8 or 12**.)*
Special Note: *If you do not have a Works Cited, you will not make more than 50% on the final paper.*	

Theme Paper Rubric		
Proficient 6-8	*Basic 4-5*	*Below Basic 0-3*
4-7 mistakes	*8-11 mistakes*	*12 or more mistakes*
Only 5-6 of the requirements in the advanced box are met.	*Only 4-3 of the requirements in the advanced box are met.*	*Only 2 or fewer of the requirements in the advanced box are met.*
Four elements of the literature are described and clearly connected to theme with specific examples from the text, or the connections of the theme to the literature aren't clear.	*Two to three elements are connected, or connections are fairly poor.*	*Only one element of literature is present, or no clear connections are made.*
• *Most references are cited.* • *Most quotes give exact page numbers (in MLA style).* • *Block quotes only have 1 mistake.* • *2-4 small mistakes on the works cited*	• *A few references are cited.* • *Quotes not all referenced* • *Block quotes are riddled with problems.* • *5-6 mistakes on the works cited page*	• *A few references are cited.* • *No quotes referenced* • *7 or more mistakes on the works cited page*
• *Intro and conclusion are short paragraphs.* • *Intro gives at least 2 pieces of information about the theme.* • *Conclusion mostly sums up the paper and gives only a bit of depth.* • *Thesis is in the intro somewhere.* • *Thesis just names the theme or just 2 main points.* • *It would be hard to outline paper with this thesis.*	• *Intro and conclusion are only 1 sentence.* • *Intro gives 1 piece of information about the theme.* • *Conclusion only sums up the paper.* • *Thesis is difficult to find.* • *Thesis names only 1 main point.* • *Cannot outline paper at all by reading this thesis.*	• *No noticeable intro or conclusion* • *No definable thesis statement*
• *A few small troubles with the flow of the sections* • *Paper is a bit choppy.*	• *Several problems with the flow of the sections* • *Paper is rather choppy.*	• *Paper feels like a random assortment in a candy dish.*
• *Final Draft is turned in on the date it is due (just not in class).* • *Final Draft is too long or too short.*	• *Final Draft is turned in by or before Monday of next week.* • *Final Draft is rather long or rather short.*	• *Final Draft later than Monday of next week.* • *Final Draft is incredibly long or incredibly short.*
Final Grade:		*/80*

Conclusion
Mark Hilliard and Jessa Sexton

Remember the chart that listed the qualities that make a teacher "good" versus those qualities that make a teacher "bad"? Though those replies were given by people unaware of the Education Wellness philosophy, the qualities of a good teacher can be attained, and those of a bad teacher avoided, through the six pedagogical elements of this approach to teaching and learning.

By integrating the experiences of the teacher and pupil, education becomes a community event—students viewing their teachers as passionate, knowledgeable, and approachable; teachers viewing their students as individuals capable of learning.

Once educators acknowledge the individual needs of their students, they must employ a multiplicity of teaching and learning styles and tap into the endless possibilities of using the senses to reach each student.

Good instructors do not limit their teaching to the facts; they engage their students in high-level critical thinking, using methods such as the Hilliard Circle of Teaching and Learning to move their students from initial connections to the opportunity of becoming an expert with the ability to teach others.

Without alternative methodologies for assessment, true learning and great teaching cannot occur. These different techniques allow students to show a mastery of skills and knowledge instead of the ability to repeat memorized facts. Also, opportunities for appropriate teacher assessments can help willing teachers meet their potential for scholastic greatness.

The environment that surrounds both the teacher and the student is an important consideration as we create true learning experiences. Some of the educational surroundings are outside of our control, but many openings abound for us to create a space that is set apart for learning, thereby encouraging our students to learn.

And, finally, we must reexamine the old-school lecture. If we already use it, how can we better do so? If we have been avoiding it, how can we successfully reincorporate it into our academic world? The lecture still has value as an educational tool, if we are willing to be more considerate and deliberate of our delivery.

By using the Educational Wellness philosophy in any school system, individualized and creative learning should flourish. With this educational formula, students should become engaged in the teaching and learning processes. New knowledge and skills become a part of the whole person rather than facts stored for rote recall. Likewise, teachers who enter the Hilliard Circle of Teaching and Learning with their students will become more engaged in the teaching processes, finding more meaning and relativity and creating passionate, informative delivery.

Teaching is not a "fall-back" job; it is an ever-inspiring, constantly challenging profession. Our desire, as fellow educators and lovers of learning, is that the ideas of Educational Wellness will inspire you to confront the temptation for mediocrity in your classroom, motivating your students—and yourself—to become lifelong learners.

References

ADA Compliance 2013: Issues in Higher Education. Little Falls, NJ: PaperClip Communications, 2012. Print.

Aristotle. "Quotes About Teaching." *Goodreads.com.* 2014. Web. 30 July 2014.

Beechick, Ruth. "Quotes About Teaching." *Goodreads.com.* 2014. Web. 30 July 2014.

Beene, Alex. E-mail Interview. 8 Jan 2015.

Bloom, Benjamin. *Taxonomy of Educational Objectives: The Classification of Educational Goals.* Boston: Allyn and Bacon, 1984. Print.

Brazas, Jeremy. E-mail Interview. 2 August 2014.

Burns, Robert. "To a Mouse." *Robertburns.org.* n.p. 1785. Web. 24 June 2012.

"Come to Your Senses." *Thinkquest.org.* 15 August 2005. Web. 2 November 2006.

Cregg, Hannah. Email Interview. 9 Jan 2015.

Davis, Stephen and Joseph J. Palladino. *Psychology: Media and Research Update.* 4th ed. NJ: Prentice-Hall, 2005. (107-113). Print.

Fraser, Barry J. *Classroom Environment.* New York City: Routledge, 2012. eBook.

Gough, Stephen. Personal Interview. 4 July 2013.

Hilliard, Jack. *Hilliard's Proverbs: Inspired By Experience.* Franklin, TN: Hilliard Press, 2013. Print.

Hilliard, Mark. *Spirit-Ritual.* Franklin, Tennessee: Hilliard Press, 2006. Print.

Hubbard, Elbert. "Quotes About Teaching." *Goodreads.com.* 2014. Web. 30 July 2014.

Illich, Ivan. "Quotes About Teaching." *Goodreads.com.* 2014. Web. 30 July 2014.

Living Well with Your Sense of Smell. New York: The Sense of Smell Institute, 1992. Print.

Manns, Shelley. Personal Interview. 22 July 2014.

Ormond, J. E. *Human Learning*. 3rd ed. Upper Saddle River, NY: Prentice Hall, 1999. Print.

Palmer, Amanda. Personal Interview. 3 July 2013.

Palmer, Parker J. *The Courage to Teach: Exploring the Inner Landscape of a Teacher's Life*. Tenth Anniversary Edition. San Francisco: Jossey-Bass, 2007. Print.

Shakespeare, William. *Romeo and Juliet. The Complete Works*. New York: Gramercy Books, 1975. Print.

Smith, Lesley. Personal Interview. June 2007.

Spirituality in Higher Education: A National Study of College Students' Search for Meaning and Purpose. Los Angeles: UCLA Higher Education Research Institute, 2006. Print.

Steinbeck, John. *The Pearl*. New York: Penguin Group, 1976. Print.

"Tutorials." *Oxford Magazine* 265 (2007):20-22. Print.

Ward, William Arthur. "Quotes About Teaching." *Goodreads.com*. 2014. Web. 30 July 2014.

Weimer, Maryellen. *Enhancing Scholarly Work on Teaching and Learning*. San Francisco: Jossey Bass, 2006. Print.

Wilde, Oscar. "Quotes About Teaching." *Goodreads.com*. 2014. Web. 30 July 2014.

Young, Dolly Jesusita. "Creating a Low-Anxiety Classroom Environment: What Does Language Anxiety Research Suggest?" *The Modern Language Journal* 75.4 (1991): 426-37. Online.

Zinsser, William. *On Writing Well: The Classic Guide to Writing Nonfiction*. New York: Collins, 2006. Print.

About the Authors

Mark Hilliard D.Arts (Doctor of Arts)

Hilliard's doctoral training includes an emphasis in higher education that deeply embraces the *art and philosophy* of teaching and learning, but he specialized in wellness—a field of *science* which includes psychology, physiology, sociology, and the metaphysical field of spirituality. As such, he trained in both the arts and the sciences and believes these two disciplines complement each other and that they necessitate unity in order for higher learning to occur. Hilliard believes, "When appropriately joined together, the art and science of teaching and learning create *educational wellness*." Professor Hilliard's training also includes years of research into Native American cultures and learning styles (specifically the Eastern Band of the Cherokee and the Lakota) that highly incorporate individualized sensory, intuitive, and spiritual philosophies of teaching and learning.

Because of his scholarly research, in the summer of 2006, Dr. Hilliard was invited by the Oxford Round Table, Jesus College, University of Oxford, England, to present his research on Educational Wellness (specifically his *Hilliard Circle of Teaching and Learning Theory*) before a group of forty educators from around the world. He returned to the University of Oxford, Harris Manchester College, as a Visiting Research Scholar and Fellow in June 2007, 2010, 2013, and 2014 to further his studies on sensory teaching and learning.

Dr. Hilliard served as President and CEO of O'More College of Design in Franklin, Tennessee, and was a distinguished professor of Educational Wellness, Marriage and Family, Holistic Wellness, and Spirituality. He is currently the Vice Chancellor, President, and Professor of The Hilliard Institute; Visiting Fellow, Harris Manchester College, University of Oxford; and Director-General, The Oxford Centre for the Study of Law and Public Policy.

Jessa R. Sexton M.Ed.
(Masters of Education)

In kindergarten, Jessa knew she wanted to be a teacher. Basing her early decision on a desire to write on the chalkboard whenever she pleased, Professor Sexton has now developed a more sophisticated educational drive. At Harding University, she received a bachelor of arts in English with teacher licensure and a Masters of Education with an emphasis in English. During her time at Harding, she performed with the Pied Pipers, an improvisational children's theatre troupe that toured schools and churches throughout sections of America and worked one summer tour in England. This group made teaching an entertaining and relatable endeavor, a goal Sexton sets for herself in the classroom.

Her teaching experiences include student teaching seventh grade language arts and a permanent substitute position for six months in ninth grade English. As a graduate assistant in Harding's Writing Lab, Sexton tutored students from a variety of language and ethnic backgrounds; she defines this as some of the best training she received in refining her ability to teach writing skills. She also worked closely with Upward Bound, a government-funded educational resource for high school students who qualify by being low-income or first generation college students, through teaching courses on composition, literature, ACT preparation, and supplemental English during the school year and the UB Summer Academy program. At O'More College of Design, Sexton served as Executive Editor of O'More Publishing and was an assistant professor in literature, Composition I and II, communication, research, and Educational Wellness. Currently, she is Pro-Vice Chancellor, Vice President, and Professor of The Hilliard Institute; Visiting Fellow, Harris Manchester College, University of Oxford; and Executive Editor and Writer for Hilliard Press.

The Hilliard Institute for Educational Wellness

The Hilliard Institute offers sensory education programing, experiential learning, and academic research and publishing while also supporting philanthropic initiatives through fundraising and educational training and activities—all under the umbrella of the concept of Educational Wellness.

What is *Educational Wellness*? *Educational Wellness* is a holistic approach to the art and science of research, teaching, learning, and philanthropic activity. This process involves both the right and left hemispheres of the brain—using both the creative and the logical aspects of research and discovery. It is a sensory approach to teaching and learning, wherein everything we do is done for a greater cause than self-benefit. It includes the spiritual, mental, emotional, and physical aspects of life and learning.

The Hilliard Institute Mission: This sensory education, experiential learning, and philanthropic institute offers unique educational training, workshops, and events to support local, national, and global non-profits, communities, businesses, individuals, schools, and other educational and/or wellness organizations. The Institute seeks not only to assist philanthropic entities with funding, but to teach others about these organizations and, when necessary, train these entities how to become more self-sustaining.

To learn more, visit our website: www.hilliardinstitute.com